MICHAEL W. SMITH
JEFFREY D. WILHELM

Getting It Right

Fresh Approaches to Teaching Grammar, Usage, and Correctness

SCHOLASTIC

New York • Toronto • London • Auckland • Sydney
Mexico City • New Delhi • Hong Kong • Buenos Aires

Our appreciation to the publisher who granted us permission to use the excerpt as follows: "Old Florist" by Theodore Roethke. Copyright 1946 by Harper & Brothers from COLLECTED POEMS OF THEODORE ROETHKE. Used by permission of Doubleday, a division of Random House, Inc.

Cover Design: Maria Lilja
Interior Design: LDL Designs
Editor: Gloria Pipkin
Production Editor: Sarah Weaver
Copy Editor: Erich Strom

ISBN-13: 978-0-439-66933-7
ISBN-10: 0-439-66933-2

To George Hillocks Jr., who taught me to think hard
about what and how to teach

— Michael Smith

To Mr. Blaser, who first taught me about
revising and proofreading, and to all the teachers
and student teachers with whom I've worked at
West Junior High School in Boise

— Jeff Wilhelm

Contents

Acknowledgments

Michael sends his thanks to all of his Rutgers and Temple students, with whom he first explored many of the ideas that appear in this book. He sends thanks, too, to many colleagues whose thinking about language and teaching has influenced his own, especially Julie Cheville, Judy Diamondstone, Eli Goldblatt, Wallis Reid, Frank Sullivan, and Brian White. All of Michael's work has its genesis in the training he received from George Hillocks Jr. at the University of Chicago. George sent Michael down the path that culminated in this book when he hired him to read and review the grammar studies that George analyzed in *Research on Written Composition*. Michael's UC colleagues, especially Steve Gevinson, Larry Johannessen, Betsy Kahn, Carol Lee, Steve Littell, Tom McCann, and Peter Smagorinsky, push him by their example to think about instruction that fosters deep understandings in students. Thanks to all.

Jeff acknowledges, with a sincere salute, the work of all his University of Maine and Boise State University students and student teachers who participated in the teacher research/error analysis and intervention studies. He's particularly grateful to Denise Braswell and her CSI (Correct Sentence Investigator) Project, and to Amy Hennig, Greg Wilson, and Steven (the Monk) Wells. Jeff's students studied and used the most excellent books on grammar teaching written by Jeff Anderson (*Mechanically Inclined*) and Edgar Schuster (*Breaking the Rules*), and all of us are indebted to their insights.

Thanks also go to Rich Webb, the principal at West Junior High School in Boise, and all of the wonderful teachers there for their progressive teaching, openness, support of new ideas, and deep caring for their students. Special thank-you-grams go to Ruthanne Beddoe, Tessa Partridge, Marion Workman, Cheryl Gratton, Travis Lynn, Pam Sleney, Karen Knudtsen, and many others. Thanks also to the Boise State Writing Project fellows who contributed their thoughts to this project, among them Debbie Moore, Marion Workman, and Frank Dehoney. Speaking of the Writing Project, Jeff's approach to writing has been entirely informed by his 25 years of association with the National Writing Project, first as an attendee at workshops, then as a fellow, and now as a founding director of two sites, one in Maine and one in Boise, Idaho. The thinking of many National Writing Project fellows from around the nation has shaped the ideas in this book. Jeff is grateful in particular for his time with the Maryland Writing Project and the help given him by Elyse Eidman-Aadahl, Gloria Neubert, Michal Makarovich, and Don and Jenny Killgallon.

Finally, we'd both like to thank the people who matter most to us: our wives and daughters. We've learned so much about teaching that works and teaching that might not work so well by looking over the shoulders of Catherine and Rachel Smith and Fiona and Jasmine Wilhelm. We test our ideas by thinking about what they'd mean for our kids. Our amazing wives, Karen Flynn and Peggy Jo Wilhelm, have encouraged us to do work that matters in the world and not just in the academy and have supported us when that work sometimes took us away from home. We couldn't have done it without you. Nor could we have done it without the help of our editors at Scholastic. Gloria Pipkin was wonderfully supportive in helping us develop the manuscript, and she went above and beyond the call of duty in helping us meet our deadline. Sarah Weaver, with an invaluable assist from copy editor Erich Strom, did a great job of preparing the work for publication. Our thanks to all!

Foreword

The teaching of writing has come a long way in the past 30 years. As it has evolved from workbooks that asked students to correct sentences they did not write, to classes where students learn by writing extensively, the question of grammar and how it should be taught has been a subject of debate.

In the 1980s, the movement to help teachers and students understand the processes behind composition led to a strong emphasis on the creation of the first draft, with little attention to grammatical correctness. Subsequent drafts were written to improve coherence and logic, to help writers make their meaning clear, and finally to work toward a piece of "public" writing.

The purpose of instruction in grammar is ultimately to guarantee the clearest communication and the fullest representations of the complexities of thought, and to ensure cohesion. Achieving correctness is an essential step in the writing process. Without correctness, everyone would agree, meaning is obscured.

The questions of when, where, and how grammar should be taught are at the center of the debate. Some believe it should be taught as a discrete set of definitions and rules, with sample sentences that model the principles being taught. Others maintain that grammar and correctness should come at the penultimate stage of the writing process. Neither has been satisfactory.

Research on writing in the last 20 years has shown that grammar instruction in isolation from a student's own composition has little or no impact on the quality of the writing produced. Similarly, leaving grammar instruction until the final stages of the writing process truncates the learning—students often fail to learn the fundamentals of grammar for future writing. This is the problem that Michael Smith and Jeff Wilhelm have set out to solve.

Getting It Right: Fresh Approaches to Teaching Grammar, Usage, and Correctness takes into account this dilemma and offers teachers a set of guidelines and examples of a rigorous and powerful way to integrate instruction in grammar throughout the many stages of the writing process. Professors Smith and

Wilhelm have achieved a small miracle. The book is organized in a way that does not simply tell teachers what to do, but rather sets out the argument, demonstrates through research the soundness of the approach, and then provides examples of lessons for a variety of writing tasks, purposes, and audiences. Further, Smith and Wilhelm provide strategies for helping students meet the requirements of state assessments.

Teachers are asked to think about the argument presented, consider examples of the authors' theory of action in the classroom, and use these examples as a starting place to develop their own theory of action. Respect for teachers' knowledge is present throughout, and the authors' approach encourages us to respect student learning in the same way. Meta-analysis is a powerful tool to help teachers understand why they do what they do, and Smith and Wilhelm enable us to see how such an approach can be equally helpful for students.

Teachers will find in this book a rich array of materials, strategies, and, even more important, an underlying theory of action that will serve them for many years. With the help of books such as this one, our profession grows stronger and we become better able to negotiate the changing landscape that affects each generation of students. Michael W. Smith and Jeffrey D. Wilhelm's contribution to the evolving professional dialogue about teaching grammar is strong evidence of the richness and importance of intellectual and professional communities, like the National Writing Project, that provide the forum for such profession-long discussions.

When I first read the title, I wondered whether a new book on teaching grammar would have the usual reception—rejection by some and acceptance by others, depending on their beliefs about the place of grammar in the teaching of writing. This book is different; it will, I predict, appeal to any teacher of writing. It takes seriously a problem for which we have had no satisfactory answers, and it gives teachers a framework for helping students take charge of their own writing to achieve both coherence and correctness. This is a book that offers common ground where professionals on both sides of the grammar debate can agree. It is both needed and welcome.

Richard Sterling
National Writing Project
University of California, Berkeley
April 2007

Chapter 1

The Elephant at The Party

Imagine the scene: You're sitting next to a stranger on a long cross-country flight. Talk turns to what each of you does for a living. "I'm an English teacher," you say. Think now of all of the possible responses you could get to that statement: "Great, my favorite subject was English!" Or "It must be wonderful having a job that's so involved with reading and writing." Or "I've always loved reading, thanks to my English teachers." Or "Writing is such an important part of my job. I learned to like it and be good at it in my English classes."

We ride lots of planes and have engaged in lots of conversations with fellow passengers. But, sadly, we very seldom receive any of the above responses when we say what we do for a living. What we do receive is something like the following: "Oh, I guess I'd better watch my English then." It seems that in the minds of the public, being an English teacher means being a member of the language police.

Recently, each of us had experiences that brought this sad truth home to us, a truth made even sadder by the fact that many teachers seem to embrace the role of English teacher as language guardian and red-pen wielder. When Michael was working with the faculty of a small middle school on using portfolios, he took the position that the faculty had to be committed to teaching whatever kinds of writing they wanted students to include in their portfolios.

He argued that teaching writing means much more than simply assigning it and then assessing it, a typical mode in American schools. He then sketched out a sequence of activities that teachers could use to teach their students to write the kind of problem-solution papers that were part of the state's writing assessment. The teachers were interested, but there was an undercurrent of resistance. After some talk Michael discovered its source: Teachers were afraid that doing a carefully sequenced unit of instruction would take too much time away from all the other things they had to do. More probing revealed their fear that such a unit would take time away from teaching grammar, and they worried that taking any time from the teaching of grammar would do their students a disservice.

"Teaching writing means much more than simply assigning it and then assessing it."

Last year Jeff's daughter Fiona had her first year in a new school system. Fiona loves to read and write, so Jeff was expecting that English would be her favorite subject. It wasn't. Day after day Fiona trudged home with work sheets on which she had to do such things as identify parts of speech, underline participles, and determine the function of different kinds of infinitive phrases. "They don't even know me, Dad," she complained. "I've been in school a semester and nobody knows me because all we do is sit in rows and fill out work sheets!"

Then Fiona came home with a review packet for her semester exam. The packet contained eight pages of multiple-choice questions about language usage and the writing process. The rich procedures of expert writing had been reduced to snippets of information for easy testing. These strategies and conventions had been removed from the writing situations in which they could be meaningful and actually used. Even more distressing was that language use had been turned into "sound bites" that had been dumbed down so they in no way matched what real authors do when they write.

For example, one question gave five possible ways to complete this sentence: During the revision process you should (A) correct your spelling, (B) word process your document, (C) complete a graphic organizer, (D) correct your grammar, (E) separate your ideas into single idea paragraphs. Between us we've written more than 20 books and well over a hundred articles or chapters. None of these alternatives describe what we as real writers do when we revise. (The correct choice was E.) Equating revision, a process through which authors sub-stantively change, add to, and rearrange their ideas, with any of the alternatives listed is not only silly but also counterproductive. What incentive would Fiona have to seriously consider her writing if all she was expected to do was reformat what she had already written? The question violates the rules of real writing and promotes an idea used only in school. When Jeff asked Fiona how this test would help her correct run-on sentences or revise more effectively, she said, "I'd learn more about that by writing an actual paper." She was undoubtedly right, and yet she had written only one paper all semester.

The next time she *was* given an extended writing assignment (a science lab), she took the opportunity to show something of herself. Instead of a report of the experiment she and her classmates did, Fiona turned in a multigenre commentary on science in general and the experiment in particular—complete with cartoons, jokes, and autobiographical incidents. She received a zero and the comment "Incorrect Lab Report Format" (a gratuitous comment, since she had of course been completing her previous reports in the correct format for over a semester).

Teaching for Correctness *and* Meaning

The purpose of this book is to help you think about the most effective contexts for and means of teaching grammar, which we've come to think about as the elephant at the party. What we mean is that although grammar is such a big part of the curricular considerations of so many schools, teachers often pretend not to notice it. Both of us write, teach, and give presentations about what we see as more effective and engaging ways to teach reading and writing. But we've come to understand that unless we address the teaching of grammar in a wide-awake way, the kind of reforms that we've been advocating will never be real-ized, for there just won't be the time and energy to enact them.

In this book we want to share briefly what research has taught us about the teaching of grammar and then to share much more extensively the research-based principles that have guided our practice of teaching correct language use. We will argue that correctness is best taught when it is in the service of helping students be more engaged and powerful readers, writers, and learners. At each juncture we'll discuss how different teachers in different situations might put those same principles into practice to meet goals for student writing and language use, both in school and out in the world.

Before we turn to the research, we first want to offer an assurance and then a definition. First, the assurance: We recognize that helping our students write more correctly is important. It's important for all of us who stake our identities and credibility on what we write. It's important for students taking high-stakes tests. It's important on the job. It's important to getting a hearing in a public forum. Although we'll be arguing that traditional approaches to the teaching of grammar are counterproductive, we won't be arguing that correctness, the goal of those approaches, is unimportant.

Second, the definition: One of the reasons that discussions of grammar are so difficult is that people mean different things when they use the term. Indeed, Hartwell (1985) has identified five different meanings for the word *grammar*. For our purposes, two meanings seem especially germane: first, the systematic description, analysis, and articulation of the formal patterns of a language, and second, a set of rules describing a standard of correctness for speaking and writing.

It's important to note that there are a variety of grammars and various schools of linguistics that seek to provide a systematic description of the way that language works. Structural Grammar, Transformational-Generative Grammar, Columbia School Linguistics, and Systemic Functional Linguistics are all examples. The grammar that most of us are familiar with is called Traditional School Grammar (TSG). TSG seeks to provide a description of the language through the analysis of the function of words and clauses. The vocabulary of TSG is one with which we're all familiar: the eight parts of speech, each of which has a number of different classes; the parts of a sentence (e.g., subject, predicate, object); different kinds of phrases (e.g., prepositional, participial), clauses (e.g., adverbial, relative), and sentences (e.g., simple, compound); and verb tenses and moods. The list could continue. Other grammars tend to borrow some terms from TSG and to add others of their own (e.g., the *kernel* in Transformational-Generative Grammar or *theme* and *rheme* in Systemic

Functional Linguistics). But despite that borrowing, different grammars have different theoretical suppositions, purposes, and modes of analysis. When we say TSG, we mean the teaching of an analytic system to describe the function of words. Typical TSG activities include labeling words and groups of words in sentences and diagramming sentences.

In contrast, when we focus here on teaching correctness, we mean something quite different: activities that are more immediately directed toward bringing student writing and/or speaking in line with what is called Standard American English. Instruction in correctness includes both issues of usage (e.g., the difference between *less* and *fewer*) and punctuation, and is best conducted in the context of our students' own disciplinary inquiries, reading, and writing.

The Plan for This Book

In Chapter 2, we'll discuss what lessons teachers can learn from the research on teaching grammar and correctness. It's our contention that teachers are professionals, and that as such we should know the research base regarding what we teach. This is important for several reasons: so that we can be informed, wide awake, and critical about our own practices; so that we can engage in policy discussions; and so that we can work for changes in our own school policies, curriculum, and assessment practices.

Beginning in Chapter 3, we'll talk about what we see as important principles in helping students write more correctly. First, we'll argue that errors matter but all errors do not matter equally—and many do not matter nearly as much as we think they do. We'll talk about the importance of developing a hierarchy of errors. This hierarchy will help us know what to pay attention to and how to sequence attention to significant errors both within and across classes of students. We'll also argue that students must be assisted to research and track their own language use and improvement. As part of our discussion of the hierarchy of errors, we'll focus on the importance of considering the cost of correcting them, both in terms of instructional time and in terms of students' feelings of self-efficacy.

> "Errors matter but all errors do not matter equally—and many do not matter nearly as much as we think they do."

In Chapter 4 we'll differentiate performance-based and knowledge-based errors. We'll argue that most errors happen for a reason and that it's impossible to correct such errors simply by noting their existence. We'll discuss some common causes of errors and approaches we've found successful in dealing with them. In this chapter we will also explain why we think that students must learn to inquire into language use and its effects in the context of their reading and writing, and that our job is to assist them (i.e., to model, mentor, and monitor students [Wilhelm, 2007]) in constructing new conceptual and procedural understandings that can be applied to appreciating, responding to, and using language.

In Chapter 5 we'll summarize the approach we've advocated. And we'll test that approach against the reality of high-stakes standardized tests.

In short, in this book we will explore language use by considering what is truly important to teach and how to teach those things in a context that matters to students "in the here and now," a phrase we borrow from a student who was talking about the kind of instruction and assignments he found motivating.

Here goes.

Chapter 2

What We Know and What It Means

Michael's wife is a lawyer. One of the frustrations of her job has been working with professors who are expert witnesses. "The problem with professors," she complains, "is that they never come right out and say anything point-blank so a jury can understand them. They always want to complicate and qualify what they're saying." Indeed, as educational researchers, we're taught to look for the limitations of our own work and to share those limitations with our audience. Perhaps that's why it's so striking when a respected researcher makes an unequivocal claim.

What the Research Says: The Curious Case of the Unequivocal Finding

In the past 50 years or so, there have been two comprehensive reviews of research on the teaching of writing. And each has made an unequivocal claim about the teaching of grammar. Braddock, Lloyd-Jones, and Schoer (1963) made this declaration:

> The teaching of formal grammar has a negligible or, because it usually displaces some instruction and practice in actual composition, even a harmful effect on the improvement of writing. (pp. 37–38)

Twenty-three years later, Hillocks (1986) offered an equally strong assessment:

> School boards, administrators, and teachers who impose the system-
> atic study of traditional school grammar on their students over
> lengthy periods of time in the name of teaching writing do them a
> gross disservice which should not be tolerated by anyone concerned
> with the effective teaching of good writing. (p. 248)

Both comprehensive reviews base their claims on a careful analysis of a wide range of studies on the teaching of grammar. Recent reviews that focus exclusively on the teaching of grammar (Hillocks & Smith, 2003; Smith, Cheville, & Hillocks, 2006) echo their findings. Rather than attempting to duplicate those reviews and inundate you with the sheer number of studies that have been done (the Hillocks and Smith review has 117 bibliographic entries), we thought it would make sense to focus in greater depth on the single study that seems to us to be the best of the bunch.

That study was done in New Zealand by Elley, Barham, and Wyllie in 1976. They examined the achievement of New Zealand high school students over four years, three of which included the pursuit of a single instructional treatment, and then a follow-up one year later. Students (248 at the outset and 166 after three years) were divided into eight classes matched on the basis of sex, ethnicity, contributing school, subject option, and four test scores. Three of these groups studied the Oregon curriculum for three years, which included Transformational-Generative Grammar (TGG), one alternative approach to the teaching of grammar that was popular at the time. Three other groups studied extra literature and creative writing instead of grammar instruction. The final two groups studied Traditional School Grammar (TSG). The instruction in literature for all of the classes was centered on the study of six to eight sets of popular fiction. The researchers used a variety of measures after each year of the study: tests of reading, listening, English usage, spelling, English literature, and sentence combining; the analysis of essays the students had written; and attitude surveys.

With students getting such different curricula for such a long time, one might expect to see significant differences on a variety of measures. However, the findings are notable for how few differences were found. At the end of the first year, no significant differences among groups existed on any of the measures. At the end of the second year, the TSG group's essay content was significantly better than the no-grammar group, and the TGG group's attitude toward writing and literature was significantly worse than the other two groups. At the end of the third year, the TGG group and the no-grammar group performed significantly better on the sentence combining test. Both grammar groups performed significantly better on a standardized English usage test. However, there were no significant differences in the quality or correctness of students' actual writing. Even the difference on the usage test that favored the grammar groups doesn't seem to be a reason for much cheer because it "was dispersed over a wide range of mechanical conventions, and was not clearly associated with sentence structure" (Elley et al., 1976, p. 15). Moreover, this advantage must be weighed against the negative effect of studying grammar on students' attitudes toward English. Elley and his colleagues report that both grammar groups found English less "interesting" than the no-grammar group.

What might account for the fact that study after study has found that teaching TSG has a negligible or even negative effect on students' writing? One reason is that students just don't seem to learn grammar. We've talked to lots of students over the years, and a very common complaint is that they get the same grammar instruction in class after class. We've talked to lots of teachers over the years, and a common complaint is that they have to teach grammar over and over because their kids don't come to them knowing it, despite the efforts of their colleagues in prior years. Even our English methods students at the university profess not to have learned much about grammar from all their years of instruction.

This isn't a recent phenomenon. The most compelling study that makes the point that students have difficulty learning TSG is an old one. Macauley (1947) presented Scottish students of varying academic levels sets of sentences and asked that they identify the nouns, verbs, adjectives, and adverbs. He administered the test to 131 students who had completed primary school with 30 minutes of grammar instruction daily for four years. With passing set at 50 percent, only one student passed. Thirty-seven percent passed on nouns, 21 percent on verbs, and only 5 and 4 percent passed on adjectives and adverbs, respectively. He administered the same test to students completing the elite senior secondary school, which, in Scotland, admitted only the top 20 percent of junior secondary school graduates. These students had studied grammar for nine years. Of these top students only 42 percent were able to identify 50 percent of the items correctly.

A couple of things seem especially striking to us. First, Macauley simply asked students to identify parts of speech. He didn't ask them to make any of the finer discriminations that TSG allows, for example, among reflexive, relative, interrogative, demonstrative, and indefinite pronouns. Second, it appears that there weren't any good old days when, by God, kids learned their grammar.

Maybe one reason students have difficulty learning even such seemingly simple grammatical ideas as the parts of speech is that traditional grammatical definitions don't take into account the complexity of language in use. Turning quickly to the old *Warriner's English Grammar and Composition: Third Course* book (1982) that Michael used when he was teaching provides an illustration. The first term that the book introduces is the noun, "a word used to name a person, place, thing or idea" (p. 4). The book goes on to provide five or six illustrations of each class of noun. And at least one example in each of the lists is at least somewhat problematic. The list of persons includes "hair stylist." But couldn't *hair* be regarded as an adjective modifying *stylist*? The list of places includes "kitchen." What then to make of a kitchen knife? The list of things includes "money." What to make of a money player or a basketball player who shouts "Money!" after releasing a shot he or she knows to be good? The list of ideas includes "strength." How about a strength coach?

The following table sketches some definitional problems that might make learning the parts of speech difficult.* We hope that these few examples illustrate the complications that arise when one tries to apply straightforward

---

* As Kolln and Funk (1998) point out, modern structural grammarians would reject the traditional list of eight parts of speech and replace it with form classes and structure classes. Form classes are large classes of words that can be defined by the systematic changes that are possible for words of a given class. In structural grammar, for example, nouns are defined as those words that are able to take a plural and a possessive, adjectives are words that have both a comparative and superlative form. They identify four form classes (nouns, verbs, adjectives, and adverbs). Structure classes "explain the grammatical or structural relationships of the form classes." According to Kolln and Funk, they include determiners, auxiliaries, qualifiers, prepositions, conjunctions, interrogatives, expletives, and particles.

Getting It Right

Problems With the Parts of Speech

	Common Definition	Potential Problems
Noun	Name of a person, place, thing, idea	Many words that are typically nouns can have other functions in other sentences. *Floor*, for example, can be an adjective (*floor wax*) or a verb (*The boxer floored his opponent*). Pronouns also name a person.
Verb	A word that expresses action or state of being	Students have difficulty understanding what "state of being" means. Words that are verbs in one context can have other functions in other sentences (e.g., *fish*). Participles are some-times principal parts of verbs, but they are adjectival on their own. Present participles are the same form as gerunds, which work as nouns.
Pronoun	A word that takes the place of a noun	The definition also fits synonyms. Many words that are often pronouns (e.g., *this*) are used as adjectives in other contexts.
Adjective	A word that describes or modifies a noun	Words that are often adjectives can have other functions in other sentences (e.g., *solid*). The definition also fits possessive pronouns. Articles are adjectives, but they don't really modify or describe nouns.
Adverb	A word that modifies verbs, adjectives, and other adverbs	Most adverbs end in –*ly*, but many words ending in –*ly* are typically adjectives (e.g., *friendly*).
Preposition	A word that shows the relationship of a noun or pronoun to some other word in the sentence	Every word in a sentence is related in some way to one or more words. The definition makes sense only to people who already know it. Words that are typically prepositions can have other functions, especially when they work in concert with other words (for example, *of* in the sentence *I kind of thought we'd be finished by now*). Complex prepositions are more than one word long.
Conjunction	A word that joins words or groups of words	Coordinating conjunctions work differently than do subordinat-ing conjunctions. Subordinating conjunctions may introduce an initial clause rather than join two clauses. The definition would also appear to fit prepositions and relative pronouns.
Interjection	A word that shows excitement or emotion	The definition works for any exclamation. Many common inter-jections are more than one word long and contain words that are not interjections when used by themselves (e.g., *Good lord!*).

definitions even to what appear to be the easiest of grammatical concepts. The complications increase as the concepts increase in difficulty. For example, infinitives are a verb form usually preceded by *to*, but not always—base or zero infinitives don't include *to*. Infinitives are used as nouns, adjectives, and adverbs, but they may also have a subject. Hmm. Plus, not having an immediate need and functional use for something undermines learning it. The need and use for most grammatical terms doesn't extend beyond school. If students have difficulty learning grammatical terms, we think we understand why.

But even if students learned all of the terms and could identify them in sentences and place them in diagrams, it's not likely that their knowledge would help them write more effectively. The purpose of TSG is analysis. Writing, in contrast, is a synthetic activity. Just as taking apart a clock that someone else designed and put together doesn't mean that you can make a clock, taking apart and labeling sentences of someone else's construction doesn't mean that you can construct comparable sentences on your own. Moreover, paying attention to grammatical forms and rules diverts attention from structuring coherent prose. Hartwell (1985) provides a striking example. He asked a variety of people, from sixth graders to high school teachers, to cite the rule for ordering adjectives of age, nationality, and number in English. No one was able to do so. However, when he asked those same people to put the words in the phrase "French the young girls four" in order, *all* native speakers very quickly produced "the four young French girls." When he provided the rule for using the definite article, the indefinite article, or no article and asked native speakers to apply it in a passage in which the articles were deleted, he found that most native speakers reported "a great deal of frustration." They got so bollixed up trying to follow the rule that they made mistakes. Hartwell's studies suggest that the grammatical intuitions of native speakers trump their conscious attempts to apply grammatical nomenclature. So learning grammatical rules can actually undermine correct usage!

So What to Do?

That's not to say that we think no TSG terms should be taught. If we want to talk with our students about writing well and writing correctly, we need to have some common vocabulary. It is to say, however, that we need to think hard both about the number of terms that we teach and the way that we teach them. Otherwise, as the data make clear without qualification, we will expend tremendous energy and student time with no or negative effects.

What to Teach

Let's start by thinking about the number of terms we need to teach. It seems to us that there are only two justifications for teaching a term:

1. The term is so commonly used that teachers, texts, and tests presume that students know it.
2. The term is essential to being able to explain an important issue of style or correctness.

Let's apply these criteria to some commonly taught terms. *Noun* seems to us to make the cut on the basis of the first criterion and *proper noun* might make it on the basis of the second (though one could probably get by teaching capitalization conventions using the term *name* instead of *proper noun*). Sometimes simpler terms are more useful to students than official, formal terminology. For example, use *name* instead of *proper noun* or *logical linker* instead of *adverbial conjunction*. But we can't for the life of us see why anyone would ever need to know the difference between abstract and concrete nouns. Nothing one does with a noun depends on knowing that distinction.

We think *pronoun* makes the list along with *antecedent* because students have to be able to make the relationship between pronouns and antecedents clear if their writing is to be understood. But we can't understand why it would be important to make distinc-

> "Sometimes simpler terms are more useful to students than official, formal terminology. For example, use *name* instead of *proper noun* or *logical linker* instead of *adverbial conjunction*."

tions among reflexive, relative, interrogative, demonstrative, and indefinite pronouns. *Subject* and *predicate* make the list because of their importance in students' developing a sentence sense (more on that in the next chapter), but we don't think *complement* does. Complements are seldom implicated in a correctness issue. Moreover, we'd argue that saying "That's them" instead of "That's they" at the arrival of a group of friends or "I feel badly" instead of "I feel bad" when one is expressing remorse isn't a very significant error (more on that in the next chapter as well), certainly not worth the time or effort to have students distinguish among the four types of complements. Rather than teach students all the verbals, we'd focus only on participles, as using participles is a useful technique for descriptive writing. (We'll talk about how we do this in the next section of this chapter.)

We wouldn't teach infinitives because they don't seem to us to be germane to discussions of style (we've never said, "Boy, this paper could use a few infinitives!") and infinitives aren't implicated in any correctness issues. Similarly, it doesn't make sense to us to teach gerunds because, once again, gerunds are only important in discussions of style when one is talking about parallelism, and on those occasions it's easy enough to help students see how items in a series should be the same kind of word, phrase, or clause without requiring them to know the names of all the kinds of words, phrases, and clauses they might use. Moreover, the only correctness issue that involves gerunds is that gerunds take possessives, a rule that seems to be broken at least as much as it's observed. So even if students were to learn the terms, a questionable assumption at best, it doesn't seem worth the time to teach some of them.

Here's the list of terms we'd teach: the eight parts of speech; subject and predicate; passive and active; singular and plural; phrase, clause, and sentence; compound; agreement; antecedent; and participle. We think they meet one or both of the criteria we discussed. Our list is on the short side, we realize, and it's possible that we may have neglected a key term or two, but that's okay. If a term becomes essential to the work of a class, you can always teach it at that point. And if the need never arises, well, there's the proof that it wasn't important.

Terms We'd Teach

- Noun
- Verb
- Pronoun
- Adjective
- Adverb
- Preposition
- Conjunction
- Interjection

- Subject and predicate
- Passive and active
- Singular and plural
- Phrase, clause, and sentence
- Compound
- Agreement
- Participle
- Antecedent

When Jeff's student teachers studied (over the past three years) the correctness issues that caused middle schoolers' "high-cost errors"—that is, significant communication or authority problems in their writing—they found that the list we have proposed was more than sufficient for helping students to both understand and correct these errors. They also found that the students with whom they worked understood these terms or could easily be helped to understand them, whereas other terms such as *infinitive*, *gerund*, *appositive*, and the like were opaque and often frustrating to students, even after significant instructional time had been spent on them.

As we'll illustrate below, when we say "teach the terminology," we mean something much different from providing students with work sheets in which they are called upon to underline and label and diagram. As the research unequivocally establishes, there just isn't any kind of payoff for doing that kind of work. We mean at the same time something less and something more. That is, we think that kids need to know the definitions of a few terms, which is something less than they traditionally get. And we think that kids need to experience the importance of those terms, as much as possible, in the context of their reading and writing, which is something significantly more than students traditionally get. Rather than using terminology to label, we want students to learn the terms by using them to make meaning in their writing and/or reading, to inquire, and to explore and discuss language use issues in their own writing, that of their peers, and that of the authors they read and enjoy.

How to Teach

Our advice here is relatively simple: Teach terms that students need in order to do important work in their writing and reading by creating occasions in which students can see the necessity of the terms they're learning. The work that the terms are immediately applied to should be work that matters to students and that clearly counts in the world. Whew, easier said than done. But let's start with a specific example: the teaching of verbs.

Teaching Verbs

We think the first step in designing instruction on verbs is to apply our something less/something more formula. The something less would be to provide a simple definition: You could simply say, "Most verbs are words that show action, though some verbs, especially the verb *be* in all of its forms, are used when describing how things and people are, were, or will be." Or you could try a structural definition: "Verbs are words that change forms when you talk about the past, present, and future." We think it is a good idea to provide both definitions. It's also a good idea to post the definitions in the classroom while the students are working on verbs.

Teaching a term and definition in a context in which it will immediately be put to use gives students a reason to learn it. Such contexts include discussing and responding to a reading selection and preparing, practicing, or revising a piece of student writing—or better yet, both. The context should require students to transfer what they've learned to doing the real work of readers or writers. If real writers and readers don't use particular strategies or concepts, then they shouldn't be taught.

Pantomimes. One way to encourage students to apply their understanding of verbs is to do some pantomimes of an action that might be important to the current unit or inquiry being pursued in class or that might be helpful in the next writing assignment. So, for example, if the class were engaged in writing that involves describing character actions, you could focus on describing human movement with verbs.

You could walk briskly across the classroom like a businessperson late for an appointment. And then like a student dreading entering a class. And then like a little kid in a park, distracted by all that surrounds him or her. Small groups of students could work together to identify the most specific appropriate word for what you did (*stride*, *slink*, *meander*, etc.). They could then share, compare, and evaluate the effectiveness of their small-group choices in the larger group.

Brainstorm. After the pantomime exercise, students could brainstorm lists of words that describe different ways of walking, running, moving, gesturing, and the like. You could ask your kids to do the pantomimes of some of their choices. They could put their list on the board and then pantomime one of the verbs and have the class guess which one they are performing and why—this would also help them develop vocabulary and pay attention to details.

Thesaurus. Or you could teach students how to use the thesaurus as a way to generate more alternatives that would describe different ways of doing something. They could create vocabulary tableaux (frozen pictures created with the students' bodies, or visual depictions created with art material; see Wilhelm, 2003, 2004) demonstrating the meaning of a verb on their list, and compare their tableaux. Your kids could then work together to write sentences using one or more of the verbs they've brainstormed. A bonus would be helping students learn how to use the thesaurus in an immediately meaningful context.

Scenario Response. Another idea is to provide students with situations like this one: "It's 7:00 p.m., an hour after Joe and Sarah had promised to be home. They've been in the park with friends. Their mom has had it. She's really mad. She's on her way to the park. Joe and Sarah see her approach. Sarah's concerned. She doesn't want to get grounded. Joe knows he's done for. This is the third time this week he's been late. He's tired of his mother's always harping on him to get home."

After students imagine the scene, they can describe how each character would be moving, using one of the words the class had brainstormed. They can also create a short script with stage directions describing how the characters move. Then you can show why verb choice is important by changing the scene and asking how the mother's movements would change if she were worried instead of angry. You might also have them write from one character's perspective, as though he or she were looking back on the event.

Video Excerpts. Yet another possibility is to have the class brainstorm different verbs that have something to do with singing. Then you could show very short excerpts of *American Idol* and ask kids to choose the verb that best describes what each contestant did. Students might use these verbs to write a review of a segment of the show featuring several performers. You should encourage students to include other details in their writing that support their choice of verbs, focusing especially on the impact the singing was likely to have on the audience. If students will be writing reviews, critiques, or opinion pieces, then make the connection between verbs and critical evaluation explicit. Remember to always articulate connections to the material students are reading or writing and to explain how such choices will make a difference to communication, authority, and meaning in these situations. Otherwise, you are just doing school instead of developing functional tools that students will be able to apply effectively.

Dialogue and Inflection. An activity that works especially well if kids are writing stories with dialogue is to have them say a line of dialogue in ways that would reflect a different situation. We've used "So, this is the way it's going to be," "I thought we had an agreement," and, simply, "Stop." As kids work to describe the various ways speakers inflect the sentences, they employ a range of different but related verbs. They can provide dialogue with different verbs ("Stop!" she wailed) and ask other students to perform the quoted material as the verb suggests they should. Other students can guess what verb has been provided, leading to a discussion of how readers use verbs to imagine words, tone, emotion, inflection, and the like when they read dialogue.

Guiding Principles. In each of these lessons, kids operationalize the definition of a verb you provided, seeing why and understanding how it's important to attend to verb choice. That's the "something more" part of the equation. Before we go on, we think it's worthwhile to stress what we didn't do in the lessons we described, the "something less" side of the equation. Because we are interested in engaging kids in activities that will improve their writing, their writing is our focus. We don't suggest having them read sentences and then underline the verbs. We don't have them circle auxiliary verbs. We don't do any kind of project that only involves making lists of individual verbs. No matter how creative, projects like posters or T-shirts or that require listing words out of context are invariably problematic. *Go* is a verb, but it's also a game and a place on the Monopoly board. Michael's *Warriner's* lists 12 common linking verbs in addition to forms of *be*: *appear, become, feel, look, remain, seem, smell, sound, stay, taste, turn.* At least seven of them could serve equally well on a list of nouns. In short, we'd argue that listing and underlining is *never* an effective way to teach a grammatical term. It is important to use what is learned in an immediately meaningful way that is analogous to the ways we want students to use it in the future.

Teaching the Difference Between Active and Passive

As you saw in our discussion of the terms we think are worth teaching, we believe that the distinction between active and passive merits instructional time. We think these terms are important *and* immediately applicable for the kind of reading and writing we want our students to do.

Using Headlines and Sentence Comparisons. Rather than providing the definition at the start of the lesson, we suggest an inductive approach to this lesson, which requires the students to do the work of inquiring into language use and its effects. One way to do that is to provide groups of sentences. A dramatic way to start might be to offer a set of headlines that could accompany a story about the war in Iraq:

> American Bomb Kills 10 Iraqi Civilians
> Ten Iraqi Civilians Killed by American Bomb
> Ten Iraqi Civilians Killed
> Ten Iraqi Citizens Are Casualties

You can begin the discussion by asking students to describe the differences among the four sentences. But the key question is how those differences work. A discussion of the different effects these headlines produce will help students see the stakes of the game. You can ask students to guess the newspaper's position on the war simply on the basis of the headline it chooses or to consider which publications might choose which headlines. After the discussion, you can provide definitions of *active* and *passive*. (Thanks to Allan Luke for inspiring this idea.)

During the discussion of the four headlines, students will surely comment on how the passive voice can be used to avoid assigning responsibility. But as Haussamen (1997) points out (and the preceding clause illustrates), writers can also use passive constructions to make sure that they keep the focus where they want it. Another set of headlines would help illustrate this point:

Sox Win Another One!

Yankees Beaten Again

Sox Trounce Yanks in Extra Innings

Bronx Bombers Let Another One Slip Away

A Boston paper would be much more likely to use the first and third headlines and a New York paper the second and fourth. How do you know?

Actual newspapers provide a wonderful resource for considerations of why writers choose passive constructions. The first two pages of the *New York Times* of October 27, 2004, the day we composed the first draft of this section of the chapter, provide interesting examples. One headline reads, "Pilot Maneuvers and Training Are Cited in the '01 Queens Crash." The headline writer seems to us to have rightly chosen to emphasize an important finding rather than to stress the body (in this case the National Transportation Safety Board) that made the finding. The reason for the use of the passive in "Voices of Freedom Are Stilled by Europe's Last Dictator" as a headline for a story on the policies of Aleksander Lukashenko of Belarus seems more problematic. "Europe's Last Dictator Stills Voices of Freedom" seems to us to be more dramatic. Having students find, share, and discuss instances of newspapers' using the passive will help them become more critical readers while at the same time teaching them an important grammatical distinction. It can be especially instructive to encourage students to use the Internet to find out how different newspapers across the world report the very same event, and to then compare and critique these treatments.

Applying the Passive in Student Writing. After these discussions, students should be ready to consider the use of the passive in their own writing. Of course, what they learn can be used in composing headlines for events from their reading or in composing headlines and articles for a class newspaper exploring an essential question. They can then use their headline-writing expertise to title their own papers, journal entries, and the like, and then to incorporate the strategic use of the passive and active voice in their own analyses of reading selections and in their own writing.

We find that debating school policy is one good arena for strategic use of active and passive. Students can write about policies they'd like to see or ones with which they disagree. Jeff used the following assignment with his own ninth graders for several years.

"Our School" Writing Assignment Criteria Sheet
Fact and Opinion/Problem and Solution Paper—200 points

Woo hoo! Now, as part of our social change and social justice unit (How can we work for social justice and change?), you have the chance to weigh in on a problem that is close to home—a problem (if you can think of any—ha-ha-ha) with our beloved school!

You get to weigh in twice: first with a paper that various members of the school board and administrative team have agreed to read, and second, in a group project for which you will produce one segment of a talk show with the superintendent and principal, which we will tape for our school's television station. First, the paper . . . We will brainstorm possible problems with the school that we think can be usefully addressed. We will then classify these problems and divide them up. The final paper will meet the following criteria:

1. **TITLE**: The title is creative, original, and informative regarding the paper's content.
    5 POINTS

2. **FACTS**: All of the following points (if appropriate) are covered, and if possible, shown through quotes, statistics, examples, and scenarios:

    (a) What is the problem?
    (b) What are the physical and practical manifestations of this problem, e.g., What does it look like? Feel like emotionally? Feel like physically? Etc.
    (c) What are the consequences and ramifications of this problem? What happens when it occurs, and what other problems or issues does it cause or lead to?
    (d) Who thinks it is a problem? (% of teachers; parents, students, interesting subgroups?) This will be based on your survey results—more on this later.
    (e) Where and when does this problem occur? Under what circumstances?
    (f) What exactly is the school policy concerning or related to this problem and why is it the way it is?
    80 POINTS

3. **ORGANIZATION**: The paper is organized in the method of (circle one):

    Chronological order   Order of importance   Parts of a whole   Other

    and you can explain why the paper is organized this way.
    15 POINTS

Continues

Getting It Right © 2007 by Michael W. Smith and Jeffrey D. Wilhelm, Scholastic Professional

4. **OPINION AND SOLUTION**: A solution is proposed that indeed solves the cited problem(s), and does so in a fashion consistent with the demands of school policy, state law, and the constraints under which our school personnel work. 20 POINTS

5. **AUDIENCE CONSIDERATION**: The presentation of the solution is strategically presented to appeal to the interests and perspective of the intended audience of administrators. Do the peer reviewers recognize the strategy and believe it will be successful? Comments:

20 POINTS

6. **CREATIVE PRESENTATION**: The factual information is creatively presented from a particular insider perspective—e.g., as a New Journalism on-the-scene reporter, pollster, *20/20* reporter, a person affected by the problem.

My persona is _____ and would be effective in addressing my audience because:

I achieve and present my persona by:

20 POINTS

7. **USE OF ACTIVE/PASSIVE VOICE FOR EFFECT**: You present headers and other information in the active or passive voice and can justify your choices in terms of convincing your particular audience(s). 20 POINTS

8. **OVERALL EFFECT**: The problem and solution are forcefully and convincingly presented to this particular audience by:

Peer editor evaluation of overall effect:

20 POINTS

9. In addition, certain errors will hideously affect your incipient grade! These are errors we have studied and practiced and that undermine your credibility (they also appear on the state test!). Quotation errors: -10 points; apostrophe errors: -10 points; complete sentence errors: -10 points.

THE MORAL: PROOFREAD OR PERISH!
PROOFREAD OR BE PUMMELED BY PUBLIC OPINION (NOTE THE PASSIVE!)

Getting It Right © 2007 by Michael W. Smith and Jeffrey D. Wilhelm, Scholastic Professional

In constructing their arguments, students must weigh the effects of passive and active constructions. For example, a student who is advocating a prohibition on weekend homework would inevitably face a choice something like the following: "When teachers assign homework on weekends . . ." or "When homework is assigned on weekends . . ." Asking students to discuss which version they'd choose in a paper written for an audience of administrators or teachers and whether they'd make a different choice in a paper written for an audience of students, parents, or even the general public will help them see that the difference between passive and active presents an important rhetorical choice rather than just a definition they need to memorize for a test (and then forget!).

Teaching Participles

Participles made our list not because they are used in progressive tenses, but rather because they can be useful to students when they write descriptions. As Noden (1999) points out, participles help writers of narratives evoke action without requiring a separate sentence.

Showing Writing. As we compose this section of the book, it's October, and in October teachers and students often think of writing scary stories. Imagine a scene in which a narrator is approaching a scary house. A student might write: "I approached the door of the house. I was afraid." We might encourage that student writer to "show and not tell." Many times the students with whom we worked try to show by adding sentences instead of incorporating additional details into what they have already written. If the writer wants the reader to spend a long time considering the moment, those additional sentences might work just fine. But if the writer wants to capture the scene in a quick image, "Trembling and sweating, I approached the door" could do the trick. So too might "Hands trembling, face sweating, I approached the door." (Because the noun precedes the participle in each case, "hands trembling" and "face sweating" are absolutes. You could teach the term if the distinction is important to you. We don't think it is.)

The first step in our lesson is to explain to students that the class will be working on developing strategies to help readers experience the scenes the students are working to describe. One way to start is to show a film clip of someone's opening or approaching a door of what seems to be a haunted house. If a film clip isn't available, you can simply ask students to visualize the scene. Then the class brainstorms the kind of details that would make that scene scary. The look of the door, the sound of the door, and the physical sensations the character experiences are certain to make the list.

As a second step, you could provide students with a set of descriptions of the scene that provide those details in different ways and ask them to assess their effectiveness. If it's still the Halloween season, we might provide this set of descriptions:

> ▶ The door opened slowly. It made a creaking noise that sent shivers up my spine like when I hear fingernails scraped on a chalkboard. When it opened, it scattered the cobwebs that connected it to the porch.
> ▶ Creaking so that it sent shivers up my spine, the door opened, scattering the cobwebs that connected it to the porch.
> ▶ The door opened, hinges creaking, scattering the cobwebs that connected it to the porch.

We haven't tried to stack the deck for this discussion by presenting one alternative that's clearly better than the others. Multiple sentences slow the reader down, we think, and provide the writer a chance to include more details without writing overly complex sentences. The second and third sentences both provide the image more quickly, but they have different focuses. The second sentence foregrounds the sound while the third foregrounds the door. We think it's interesting to consider whether the aural or visual appeal is more effective to more readers. Additionally, in the second sentence the sound detail introduces the sentence, while in the third it interrupts the sentence. It would be easy to throw additional considerations into the mix—for example, whether students' rankings would change if the door were described more fully (e.g., "Creaking so that it sent shivers up my spine, the heavy oaken door opened, scattering the cobwebs that connected it to the porch" vs. "The heavy oaken door opened, hinges creaking, scattering the cobwebs that connected it to the porch"). At this time it seems to us to make sense to introduce the term *participle* and to explain that it's a verb + *-ing* that's used to describe something. (We realize that participles are also principal parts of verbs, but we see no reason to introduce the term in that context as native speakers rarely misuse the principal parts of regular verbs. As Noden [1999] suggests, past participles and irregulars can be introduced later.)

After this discussion, students are ready to consider how writers use participles. You could present them with models or ask them to do some participle hunting in the scary stories they're reading (Noden, 1999). Or both. It won't take long to find them. Here's one from Poe's "The Pit and the Pendulum": "Shaking in every limb, I groped my way back to the wall; resolving there to perish rather than risk the terror of the wells, of which my imagination now pictured many in various positions about the dungeon." Here's one from "The Cask of Amontillado" (also Poe): "A succession of loud and shrill screams, bursting suddenly from the throat of the chained form, seemed to thrust me violently back." Here's one from R. L. Stine's *A Shocker on Shock Street* (2003): "With a desperate cry, I sprang to the top. Gasping for air, I pressed myself flat against the bricks" (p. 90). Stine also uses participles in less conventional ways as these stylistic fragments from *Ghost Camp* (1996) illustrate: "Opening its hairy jaws wide. Preparing to swallow us as we frantically struggled to scramble away" (p. 107).

Once students have seen how participles work, they're ready to begin appreciating their use by authors and to use them on their own. One great way to get them started is to use targeted sentence combining exercises. Sentence combining activities ask students to transform kernel sentences into ones that are more syntactically complex. Strong (1973), who has developed a corpus of instructional materials using sentence combining, defines the kernel sentence as "the basic stuff of sentences." He explains that English has between four and ten patterns of kernels, depending on the system for identifying kernels to which one subscribes. For example, the sentence with which we began our discussion of participles could be broken down into the following kernels:

The door opened.
The opening was creaky.
The creakiness sent shivers.
The shivers went up my spine.
The opening scattered cobwebs.
The cobwebs connected the door to the porch.

Asking students to combine such targeted sentences will result in a variety of sentences that the class can then analyze for their effectiveness. Daiker, Kerek, and Morenberg (1982) provide a model for the kind of targeted sentence combining that we're suggesting, though their book is designed for upper-secondary or college students.

But it's easy enough to write your own sentence combining activity by drawing on the previous writing of your students. Here is a set of combining exercises drawn from a single paragraph of a single seventh-grade student's paper (students love to use examples from their own and their classmates' papers).

I heard footsteps.
The footsteps were loud.
The footsteps were sudden.
I craned my neck.
The craning was to see.

I saw a shadow.
The shadow was of a man.
The man was well-built.
I screamed.

The man grabbed me.
The grabbing was by my neck.
The grabbing was to stop the scream.

I felt bold.
I took my elbow and jabbed.
The jabbing was at the stomach.
The stomach was of the well-built man.

I felt the blood rush.
The rushing was through my veins.
The rushing was as I struggled.

A quick look at the final set of kernels provides a sense of the kind of stylistic conversations that sentence combining can occasion. One possibility is

"Feeling the blood rush through my veins, I struggled." Another employs an absolute: "I struggled, blood rushing through my veins." Yet another: "Struggling, I felt the blood rush through my veins." Each of these choices is correct but each works in different ways. Discussing their impact on potential readers would transform a schoolish lesson on a grammar term into a toolish and functional lesson on the rhetoric of grammatical choices.

Some follow-up may be required, depending on how comfortable students have become using participles. Students can rewrite Stine's fragments into complete sentences and see whether those sentences are as suspenseful. They can find sentences in their own writing that don't employ participles and then revise them to include participles. They can rewrite sentences with participles so as not to use them. They can be given sentence combining exercises that require the use of past participles.

More Guiding Principles. What's critical is not the precise form the lessons would take, but rather the insights that guide the construction of the lessons. First, any lesson should be designed to give students tools for the writing they're currently working on, not simply to give them a term to learn. Second, students should learn terms and how to use them through extended practice in their own writing, as opposed to only doing a work sheet or analyzing someone else's writing in a textbook. (Often it's difficult to imagine that the sentences in most grammar books were written by actual flesh-and-blood writers working to communicate with flesh-and-blood readers!)

Whereas the kind of analytical exercises usually associated with TSG do not improve students' writing, the constructive exercises associated with sentence combining have a much better record. In the same comprehensive review that gave rise to his pronouncement that teaching grammar in the name of improving students' writing does them a "gross disservice," Hillocks (1986) found that "the overwhelming majority" (p. 142) of sentence combining studies done with kids as young as second graders and as old as college students demonstrate that sentence combining activities help students write more complex sentences. More important, Hillocks found that sentence combining activities resulted in significantly improved writing. Only engaging students in sequences of problem-solving activities as a prelude to writing, what Hillocks calls inquiry, proved to be more effective.

The examples we've just cited are the kinds of work we recommend doing *before* kids write. In fact, perhaps the single principle of instruction we feel most strongly

> "We need to prepare students to be successful writers rather than remediating them after they have failed."

about is that we need to prepare students to be successful writers rather than remediating them after they have failed.

As we have argued elsewhere (Smith & Wilhelm, 2006), in our experience the dominant mode of writing instruction is what we call the assign and assess method. That is, teachers assign students to do some writing and then assess that writing, hoping that the assessment will help them improve the next time. Michael's daughter Rachel just experienced a classic example. She turned in the rough draft of a research paper, and her teacher returned it, having circled every *to be* verb that Rachel used.

Unfortunately, the assign and assess method doesn't work for students or teachers. Rachel was mad because she had to rewrite her whole paper—the longest paper she had written for the class. We're sure her teacher was none too pleased, either, at the amount of time he had spent responding. Imagine, though, if Rachel's class had had some of the lesson on verbs that we have already talked about. Imagine if they had practiced working together to write a class research paper in which they used strong verbs throughout. Imagine if they had looked hard at some writing and had discussed when using *to be* verbs worked and when it didn't. Our guess is that Rachel would have used many fewer of them in her writing, so her teacher could have praised her efforts rather than tediously circling all of her mistakes.

In our research into boys' literacy (Smith & Wilhelm, 2002, 2006), we found that our informants privileged being and appearing competent above anything else. As one boy told us, "I'd rather say reading is stupid, than maybe have to admit that I might be stupid!"

If this is the case, and we are convinced that it is, then it makes sense to provide assistance to students before they attempt a new task in ways that will be generative—that is, in ways that will help students generate content and compose it in effective structures. In this way, they will be prepared and feel assured that they will develop and display increasing competence. In his work, Jeff calls this "frontloading" the reader and writer for success and engagement (see, for example, Wilhelm, Baker, & Dube-Hackett, 2001).

Although prewriting instruction is crucial, complementing that instruction with assistance *while* students write is also important. For example, when Jeff's preservice teaching students studied sixth through ninth graders' composing processes and issues of correctness, they found that specificity was one issue that was best taught both before and during the writing process, as students prepared to write and after students had written at least one draft. This way, students knew the general trajectory of their writing and the possible points and effects they were trying to achieve. They also found that focusing on correcting errors like sentence fragments, misuse of commas, and the like were best pursued after students had completed a hard draft of their writing and were ready to focus on polished correctness, rather than on what they (and we) would regard as the more important issue of content.

To conclude this chapter, we'll take up the issue of teaching specific adjectives and modifying phrases in the context of student writing. In the next chapter, we'll pick up how to teach proofreading for particular errors after the composing of content is largely complete.

Teaching Specificity

When one of Jeff's student teachers, Denise Braswell, had to teach a grammar unit (tied to both the district end-of-course exam and the state test), she wisely decided to teach the required material in the context of an inquiry into how language affects readers. As part of this unit, students wrote several descriptive pieces that helped them explore this question.

Denise decided that an important issue to address with her students, given their past writing, was that of specificity in word choice. She figured that teaching about specificity would result in a huge payoff in the quality of her students' writing as well as in their word choice scores on the state writing test. Specificity provided a means to embed instruction on parts of speech (required by the district test) in a meaningful rhetorical situation. In other words, her instruction would bear fruit in several areas: the students' writing, the students' reading, required assessments, and so on.

Denise didn't want to confuse the important issues by using too many terms, so she had to decide which ones were absolutely necessary. She then had to figure out which correctness conventions were implicated by working with specificity. For descriptive writing, she figured it would be important, in particular, to work on punctuating items in a series and combining descriptive elements. She decided to use some sentence combining activities during the drafting stages of student writing to reinforce these kinds of writerly moves at the exact time that students could use them. She wanted her students to use real dialogue and sound devices such as alliteration and rhyme in the final assignment, in which they would create a "sensorium," a New Journalistic sensory description of place, so she thought it would be effective to teach them how to use apostrophes and quotation marks during the writing process.

Menu Writing. Denise first had her students rewrite menus (see Schrank, 1979) that she had picked up from various restaurants and eating establishments around the area. In this context, students learned about using specific nouns, vivid verbs, and delicious descriptions. (As a side note, it was surprising how many of the students had never been to a restaurant and did not know how to read menus.)

Denise began her instructional sequence by having students write *something*, *anything*, *somewhere*, and *thing* on pieces of paper. She made a big deal about *thing* being a "five-letter word." Denise then had her students roll up these sheets and ceremoniously throw them in the wastebasket (some of the boys went so far as to actually destroy these overly general words!), where they were to stay "for eternity." She told the students that these words were the enemies of good writing because they lacked specificity and that she never wanted to see or hear them again. She then gave the students a list of relatively nonspecific nouns, had groups rewrite them into more specific versions (e.g., car → Toyota Prius, pet → Toto), and then write a list of nouns that became progressively more specific (e.g., pet → dog → dachshund, book → novel → *Whale Talk*).

She then asked the students to come up with the longest "sequence of specificity" that they could. For example, following is a model for a hierarchy of nouns, from the most general to the most specific:

> Transportation → land transportation → motor vehicle → car →
> Toyota → Toyota Prius → my mom's red Toyota Prius

In groups, students created hierarchies for sports, food, music, sound equipment, and human beings, among other topics, and recorded at least two of these hierarchies in their journals. They then shared and compared them in a kind of game show.

Next, groups of students completed sentences with specific nouns, using the following exercise.

Replace each underlined noun or pronoun with a more specific noun. Then try replacing one or both of the underlined nouns in each sentence with a noun phrase. You will have two new versions of each sentence.

Example:
- The <u>vehicle</u> turned left at the <u>street</u>.
- The <u>motorcycle</u> turned left at the <u>corner</u>.
- <u>Rick's 900cc Harley-Davidson</u> turned left into <u>the busy traffic of West Martin Street</u>.

Now you try these in your group:
- <u>He</u> read the <u>magazine</u>.
- <u>The rocks</u> blocked the <u>way</u> up the <u>mountain</u>.
- The <u>fish</u> swam up the <u>stream</u>.

The groups put their examples up on the board or wrote them on newsprint and taped the sheets to the wall. Each group attempted to demonstrate how its sentences were more specific and evocative than the others. In a game-show atmosphere, Denise gave points and small prizes to worthy efforts.

Next, Denise had students do the same kind of work with verbs, adjectives and adverbs, and modifying phrases. She emphasized that students' word choice should demand attention from the reader! Here's another exercise that she used.

Replace each underlined verb with a more specific verb. Then try replacing one of the underlined verbs in each sentence with a verb phrase. You will have two new versions of each sentence. First, work in groups by rewriting the following:

Example:
- Tina <u>said</u> that she had <u>seen</u> a most gruesome accident on I-85.
- Tina <u>whispered</u> that she had <u>witnessed</u> a most gruesome accident on I-85.
- Tina <u>whispered with a trembling and cracking voice</u> that she had witnessed a most gruesome accident.

Now you do it together:

- ▸ Tucker <u>walked</u> home after <u>looking over</u> his straight-A report card.
- ▸ Jilliene <u>ran</u> to catch the bus after <u>learning</u> about her basketball scholarship to Boise State.
- ▸ Brad <u>hit</u> the soccer ball into the net to <u>score</u> the team's only goal.
- ▸ The cougar <u>grabbed</u> the rabbit and then <u>ate</u> it.

After some quick work on adjectives, adverbs, and modifying phrases, the students applied all of these tools to a rewrite of their group's menu. Then they took the next week's menu for the school cafeteria and rewrote one entry to make it sound hideously unappetizing and another to make it sound like a gourmet meal from a top restaurant. For an extra challenge, the menu could be rewritten for a health-conscious parent or a member of the Department of Public Health inspection team. Here is Denise's exercise.

Monday: Ground beef patty, potatoes, peas, white or chocolate milk

Rewrite/bad: A greasy mound of chunky rat burger, gluey instant potatoes sure to plug the intestines, moldy Comet-green peas that you can use as marbles or BBs, moo juice straight from the udder!

Rewrite/good: A hefty quarter-pound of grass-fed beef cattle grilled especially for the hungry seventh-grade student, smothered in savory brown mushroom gravy, accompanied by fresh green peas straight from the pod and creamy Grade A Russet Burbank potatoes swimming in fresh dairy butter. Wash it down with a helping of fresh cold milk for healthy bones!

Tuesday: Corn dogs, tater tots, corn, white or chocolate milk
Your group's rewrites here:

Wednesday: Pizza, salad, white or chocolate milk
Your group's rewrites here:

In groups or individually, students applied what they had learned by composing their own original menu for the kind of restaurant they might like to own or run. Students were encouraged to have their menu design, food entries, and descriptions fit a particular theme. For their formal menu presentations, many groups created floor plans, models, or even example dishes for their restaurant.

Drue Hall, a drag racing enthusiast, chose the "Drag Strip Diner" for his theme, and located the fictional eatery on Fast Lane Boulevard. His creative menu featured these sections:

- First to the Line (appetizers, including "fully loaded" potato wedges)
- Fuel-Injected Entrees: Pro Stock T-Bone, Top Fuel Rib Eye, and Pro Modified Baby Back Ribs
- Blown Burgers (including the Quarter-Mile Burger)
- Hot Racing Chicks (chicken items, named for Drue's favorite female dragsters, including Erica Enders and Melanie Troxel)
- Junior Dragster (kids' menu)
- Finish Line Desserts (including Race Day Sundaes and Tire Shake Milkshakes)

Drue was motivated in part by the chance to stake his identity and interests to the rest of the class, even as he worked on his descriptive writing.

From "Blah" to "Being There." One last practice activity led directly into the final writing assignment in the instructional sequence. Denise wanted to help the students see that specific writing required them to use concrete instances instead of generalities, but she wanted them to figure this out for themselves. She began by asking students to read the two contrasting examples in the following exercise.

Blah Model:

School is boring. Teachers just talk all the time and we have to listen to them. The cafeteria food is bland and it is the same week after week. We take tests all the time and we never make or do anything.

Being There Model:

Ms. Tompkins stands in front of the classroom, behind her lectern, and clears her throat. I look at the clock. Only twenty more minutes of class! Ms. Tompkins drones on about differential equations. Joanne has her head down and is snoring. Tom, to my right, is doodling in his notebook, drawing dragons. I sigh and hold my head in my hands. At least next period is lunch. Oh joy! Corn dogs for the fifteenth Wednesday in a row!

- ▸ Which one makes you feel like you are in the school?
- ▸ How does the author achieve this effect?

Rewrite the following "blah" description into a "being there" description:

Concerts are usually great. In this one, the warm-up band played some great songs and had lots of energy. Then the lead act went out on stage. They played their top hit right off. The crowd was into it. The band played and played. Concerts can be so much fun.

Composing a Sensorium. Now students were ready to compose their sensoriums. (Jeff was introduced to this assignment by Michal Makarovich of the Maryland Writing Project.) Denise expected students to use what they had learned about descriptive writing, specific sensory details, and effective elaboration. In this way, students would apply what they had learned about grammatical concepts and terms to write in more powerful, engaging, and descriptive ways. They had fun and enthusiastically shared their work. Throughout the sequence, one activity led to another one that would exemplify and extend their previous work. After the menu and sensorium exercises, Denise engaged students as CSI (Correct Sentence Investigators) to help them proofread and polish their papers (see Chapter 4).

To begin, Denise shared three sensoriums composed by some of Jeff's former students (see Appendix C for examples and an activity featuring sensoriums). The students were asked to read the three examples, to define *sensorium*, and to list elements included in this kind of text. Their list provided the start for the list of New Journalism devices (see New Journalism Devices for Your

New Journalism Devices for Your Sensoriums

In your journal: For each device, please record a definition and an example of it from the sensoriums read in class. Work with your partners.

USES SPECIFIC INTRODUCTION AND SPECIFIC SETTING

1. Ambience—author uses lots of setting details, especially movement and dialogue, so reader will get a feeling of the place, as if she is there

USES SPECIFIC PERSPECTIVES

2. Writer is in the scene

3. Scene-to-scene movement (cinematic/camera lens—close-up, wide angle, etc.)

4. Reader is in the scene (showing versus telling)

5. Writer may address the reader intimately ("Hey, come here! Look at this! This will blow your mind!")

6. Writer may be or may use a person talking excitedly (using incompleteness, run-ons)

7. Psychological feeling—conveys how author and characters feel and are affected by the place and the action

8. Countercultural tone—expresses some tastes, values, and manners that are out of the mainstream; looks at things through a lens that is unique and provides a new angle (seeing McDonald's as a rat burger factory or a farm trough for fattening human beings for consumption by space aliens, or school as a prison for brainwashing our youth)

9. Writer uses unexpected, offbeat angles (e.g., gravedigger for Robert Kennedy's funeral, bat boy of World Series team)

10. Digression—taking off on tangents and then returning

Continues

USES SPECIFIC QUOTATIONS (WILL REQUIRE CORRECT USE OF QUOTATION MARKS)

11. Realistic dialogue (incomplete sentences, real language, informal dialect)

12. Reading people's minds

13. Sound effects (may include onomatopoeia)

14. Slang and informal diction appropriate for the setting

USES SPECIFIC AND CREATIVE DETAILS TO DESCRIBE

15. Concrete "statuspheric" details (everyday gestures, manners, habits, styles, brands that express position in the world; symbolic details—will require correct apostrophe use)

16. Metaphors and other kinds of creative comparisons

17. Figurative language (hyperbole, understatement)

18. Poetic language/sound devices (alliteration, assonance, consonance, rhyme)

19. Sensory imagery—uses all five senses

20. Repetition, parallelism, build-ups (will require correct comma use with compound and serial sentences)

21. Neologism (author makes up new words or combines words in new ways; e.g., "workadaddy," "a wellittookyoulongenough glance")

22. High-impact sentences

23. Strong action verbs

24. Connotative words (words that convey feelings and attitudes)

25. Humor—makes use of jokes, incongruities, etc.

26. Irony/sarcasm/double entendre/making snide fun of characters and places—makes use of double meanings, highlights what characters may not be aware of, might be sarcastic or judgmental

Getting It Right © 2007 by Michael W. Smith and Jeffrey D. Wilhelm, Scholastic Professional

Sensoriums). Students reread the examples and ranked the three models from best to worst. Groups justified their rankings by specifically explaining what made one better than the others. Students shared and discussed their reasoning, which became the basis of a student-generated peer editing sheet (see the Sensorium Peer Editing Sheet) and final grading criteria. In this way, students were helped to induce and articulate their own understanding of a sensorium, its purpose, its unique features, and critical standards for good ones that were subsequently used to guide and evaluate their own writing.

Sentence Combining in Context. While students drafted their sensoriums, Denise used some daily sentence combining to help them use various sentence structures, correctly punctuated, to achieve their goals and meet the assignment criteria.

As we've already explored, sentence combining is one of the few ways of improving students' stylistic sophistication and correctness. Notice that each lesson here is contextualized as preparation for or part of (e.g., the drafting stage) a particular writing assignment in a particular unit of instruction. Notice too that each assignment requires students to inquire into language construction and use and to construct, with guidance, their own understandings about rules and reasons and effects of various conventions and constructions. We have found that using examples from our students' own writing is highly effective—much more so than using canned examples. We have also found that examples that refer to students or that come from our current reading are also more engaging than the typical work sheet. The more gamelike and social the atmosphere, the more risks students will take and the more they will engage. Sherry Turkle, a psychologist at MIT, has noted what she calls the "special holding power" of gamelike structures and electronic media. So, for instance, allowing students to write their examples or contributions on strips of newsprint or on the board, fostering any kind of sharing or debate, and applying any kind of gamelike frame or action orientation, is likely to produce positive results. Finally, notice that each activity leads to immediate and repeated practice in a situation that directly leads to the students' own writing.

> "The more gamelike and social the atmosphere, the more risks students will take and the more they will engage."

Sensorium Peer Editing Sheet

For first- and second-draft peer editing:

1. Is there a title that invites the reader immediately into the lived experience of the described place?

2. Does the opening have lots of setting details, especially movement or dialogue, that immediately draw the reader into the story? Underline your three favorite details.

3. Is there one place described over a limited time?

4. Does the writing concentrate on the described place and the people there?

5. Are all five senses specifically used? Are nouns, verbs, adjectives, adverbs, and modifying phrases as specific as possible, appropriate, and deliciously different? All details must do "work" in creating associations and experiences for the reader! (Note to peer editor: If there are places that need elaboration with specific details so that the reader can see, taste, hear, feel, and smell what the writer sensed, then highlight these sections with a mark in the margin of the paper.)

6. Does the reader experience the place in a totally stimulating way, just as the writer originally did?

7. Are "statuspheric" details used to show the status life of the described people; that is, are specific symbolic possessions, gestures, actions, styles, etc. used that really reveal status and character? Star your three favorites.

8. Does the description stir up memories of similar places and people for the reader? If yes, what memories were stirred up for you?

9. Are ten New Journalism devices used to stimulate the reader and numbered in the margin? For example, scene-to-scene movement, digression, neologisms, etc.?

10. Is a sound device used? Bracket your favorite.

For editing and proofreading: Are quotes realistic and correctly punctuated? Are apostrophes used correctly? Are sentences complete (unless they are stylistic fragments)? When more than one detail is included in a single sentence, are commas used correctly? If sentences are incomplete, can the writer explain why this is effective?

Getting It Right © 2007 by Michael W. Smith and Jeffrey D. Wilhelm, Scholastic Professional

When introducing a convention of language use through sentence combining, remember these guidelines:

- ▶ Provide a meaningful opportunity for students to use what is being taught (here, to compose a sensorium of a favorite or interesting place so that readers can experience it as the writer has).
- ▶ Explicitly articulate the purpose of what is being taught (here, to generate different sentence structures for description that will provide variety and have different effects).
- ▶ Model ways you consolidate details.
- ▶ Consider the principles of good instruction in language use, including methods of getting students to inquire into and construct understandings about language usage.

Students learn language usage best under these conditions:

- ▶ They are continually doing lots of reading and writing that interests them. If the reading and writing relate to an essential question, so much the better.
- ▶ They actively inquire and construct understandings in the context of their reading and writing.
- ▶ They learn and use terminology as conceptual tools that help their real reading and writing.
- ▶ They read as writers and write as readers. That is, they read to appreciate language use and use reading as a model for trying new language constructions; they write to be read by a real audience.
- ▶ They are guided over time to more expert understandings and applications that real readers and writers use.
- ▶ They are given time, opportunity, and support to practice, take risks, and integrate what they've learned into their own writing.

Denise used the following sentence combining activities (see her lesson in the box Writing Descriptive Sentences; the work on serial sentences was adapted from fellow student teacher Amy Hennig) to help students inquire into the effects of different kinds of sentences, and to help them play with sentence variety and punctuation they could use in their drafts.

Writing Descriptive Sentences

Learning to combine sentences in our writing can be a great tool for efficiently communicating lots of ideas. Combining ideas in different ways lets writers achieve different emphases and effects. In our sensorium writing assignment, the following kinds of sentences will help you describe the place you have chosen and emphasize its qualities: how it looks, sounds, smells, and feels, and how someone might experience that place.

A Serial Sentence

Let's try some sentences that list various descriptors in a quick series.

Take a look at the three sentences below. How might you combine them into one fluid sentence using a connecting word (*and*, *but*, *or*)?

He likes tennis.
He likes baseball.   *He likes tennis, baseball, and Johnny Cash.*
He likes Johnny Cash.

What do you notice about the punctuation? How could you state a rule about how to punctuate such sentences?

The combined version is an example of a correctly punctuated sentence. Now you try this one with your partner:

She helps Shelby with her homework
She helps Sue with her horseback riding.
She helps Sally with her hopscotch.

Check yourself: Did you punctuate carefully according to the rule? How do you know you have a complete sentence? How do you know it is correctly punctuated?

What are the different emphases and effects of having the sentences separate and combining them in different ways?

Let's try another one. This one you might try on your own, if you feel confident:

On her electric guitar, Mathilda plays acid rock.
She loves to play the Rolling Stones, too.
She also likes to play songs from *JoJo*.

The Balanced Sentence

Now let's try some sentences that combine descriptions into two equal sides, like a teeter-totter with a combining word in the middle.

Sometimes you may want to combine two or three sentences that express important ideas that are a bit longer. Consider how we might combine the sentences in the following example into a balanced sentence:

She fell in love with him because he was smart.	*She liked that he treated her with respect, but she fell in love with him because he was smart.*
She liked that he treated her with respect.	

What do you notice about the punctuation? Does our rule for serial sentences still work or should we amend it in some way?

Melissa is an expert kayaker.	*Melissa is an expert kayaker, but she is not afraid to walk around a dangerous stretch of whitewater.*
She is not afraid to walk around a dangerous stretch of whitewater.	

Now it's your turn. Try this one with a partner:

Science helped him understand chemical reactions.
Science helped him see how living things are related.

Try this next one on your own—consider what sentences to combine into one half of the teeter-totter, and what should be in the other half. Think about the emphases and effects that you're trying to achieve. Think about what connecting word might be most useful.

Kayaking is exciting.
Kayaking gets you close to nature.
Kayaking can be dangerous if you do not know what you are doing.

Practice! With your partner, write a short character sketch of Mr. Wilhelm. Make sure to use at least one serial sentence (and mark it in the margin with an *SS*) and two balanced sentences (mark them in the margin with a *BS*—ha-ha).

Continues

The Parallel Sentence

Here's another kind of sentence that uses another kind of "balance," or what is called parallelism. Let's try some sentences that use parallel descriptions with verb forms, similar phrases, and so forth. Here are some examples:

> The purpose of school is <u>to help</u> students mature, <u>to prepare</u> them for work and life, and <u>to teach</u> them to be democratic citizens.

With your group, identify what is being repeated and paralleled here. Does our rule for combining elements still work?

> In the cross-country race, Fiona ran <u>into the woods</u>, <u>through the ditch</u>, <u>around a pile of wood chips</u>, <u>in between two lakes</u>, <u>across a river</u>, <u>up the hill</u>, <u>down the valley</u>, and <u>into the finish chute</u>, where she received her award.

With your group, identify what is being repeated and paralleled here. How did you feel as you read this out loud or listened? What is the effect on the reader of this kind of repetition?

Try a parallel sentence as a group. Decide what it is you will repeat. You will have to change some of the words into different forms to make it work:

> Participating in the arts and music:
>   Teamwork
>   Exciting
>   Public performances
>   Make lasting friendships
>
> Playing video games:
>   Social
>   Challenging
>   Competitive
>   Exciting

Now try one on your own.

> Going to a dance:
>   Strobe lights
>   Loud music
>   See friends
>   Dance
>   Snacks

The Build-Up Sentence

One last kind of sentence uses different parallel descriptors, but in this case it builds to a crescendo in the final phrase. Let's try some sentences that use this kind of building through parallel constructions.

> Stealing the ball, feeding passes to her teammates, grabbing loose balls and rebounds, and shooting the clutch three-pointer, Jasmine led her team to victory!

> He stirs, beats, and pours the batter into a perfect silver-dollar pancake!

> Faster than a speeding bullet, more powerful than a locomotive, stronger than gravity . . . it's a bird, it's a plane, it's Superman!

What do you notice? What is the effect and how is this achieved? Does our punctuation rule still work?

Now, as a group, construct a build-up sentence using as many repetitions as you need to give a powerful punch to the final phrase of the sentence. Choose a sentence that will work in one of your sensoriums if you can.

For final practice, on your own, rewrite the following paragraph, written with only simple sentences, so that it uses the kinds of sentences you have just practiced. You will need to justify your choices to your group, and each group will choose its most effective paragraph to present to the whole class.

> I did not want to go to Todd's party. The only food there is sushi. The only beverage is spring water. The only music is techno. He would show us his computer. He would show us his vacation videos. It was snowing. It was sleeting. The roads were covered in ice. The snow was drifting. The snow was covering the cars. I was tired. My boots leak. My coat is old. My coat is not waterproof. My coat smells when wet. I was bored. I felt guilty. Todd is my friend. Friends need to do things for each other. I went. My toes froze. I got soaked. I smelled like a cow barn. I got snowed in at Todd's house. All there was to eat was sushi. At least his house was warm.

In your final paper you should use at least one of each of the sentences we have practiced and mark it with an *SS*, *BS*, *PS*, or *BU* in the margin. You should

Continues

be able to justify your choices, and all of these sentences should be correctly punctuated!

Using Key Words

Let's say you want a shorter, punchier sentence. Another way to combine sentences is to simply pull a key word from one sentence and insert it into another. Sometimes you'll need to change the form of the key word before you insert it. Let's take a look:

Tom is a talented musician.
Tom is a rock musician.

Tom is a talented rock musician.

Now you try:

Tom would love to play for you.
Tom's instrument is a bass guitar.

Using Key Phrases

Another way to combine short sentences is to pull a key phrase from one sentence and insert it into the other. Look at the following example:

Tina enjoys hanging out with her friends.
They often meet at the arcade.

Tina enjoys hanging out with her friends at the arcade.

Now try this one:

Javon likes to read books about dragons.
Fantasy books are fun to read.

Please note that although Denise used a number of terms in her work with students, she always provided alternative vocabulary as well. Most important, students immediately put their understanding of the terms to use.

Sentence combining exercises can also be used to help students add information at the beginning of a sentence, in the middle, or at the end. New information can be added to the kernel in the form of a word (opening or delayed adjective or adverb) or phrase (such as an absolute, appositive, or participial). Again, we do not think the terms are important in these cases, with the exception of *participle*, as we don't think they help kids write more effectively or more correctly. We list them here to show a bit of the variety of sentence combining activities that are possible to do with students, in—of course—a context in which these new structures can be immediately applied.

Major Points to Take Forward

In summary, the grammatical terms that seem to us to be most important to teach are those that help students become more aware of the rhetorical choices they face in their own writing or those that help them become more discerning readers by making them aware of the rhetorical choices that other writers make. In other words, they are terms that signify ideas that are important to the real work of real readers and writers. Instruction in these terms should not consist of students' making lists of words or underlining or labeling or diagramming. Rather, students should be inquiring into the meaning and uses of the concept behind the terms, into reading and writing in contexts in which learning the terms has an immediate payoff in real activity. Such instruction not only makes it more likely that students will learn the terms, it also makes it far more likely that they will use them to become better writers and better readers. And after all, isn't that what we most want for our students?

What about correctness? We'll begin to take up that issue more directly in our next chapter. But before we do, we'd like to turn to one more question about teaching grammatical terms, one that we've already touched on but that we think is important enough to address again.

When to Teach

Our answer here is a simple one: Teach the terms that students need when they need them and when they'll use them. That answer seems so obvious that it shouldn't need to be stated, but we're afraid it does. In our work in schools, we've heard teachers defend their emphasis on grammar work sheets with some version of the following: "I have to teach them their grammar first before we move on to reading and writing because you need the basics before you move on to more advanced things."

We realize that teaching isn't a science. We realize that good teachers might have differences of opinions about what and how and when to teach different aspects of the curriculum. We realize that we risk alienating some readers by making pronouncements. But in this case we think it's worth the risk to add our voices to the unequivocal words of Braddock et al. (1963) and Hillocks (1986): *Teaching grammar as an analytical activity through labeling, underlining, and filling in the blanks does not help kids become better writers.* In fact, it hurts them because it keeps them from doing far more important things.

The knowledge of grammatical terms is *not* prerequisite knowledge. Before kids have ever encountered any grammatical terms they have constructed millions of sentences. Many linguists believe that what Schuster (2003) calls the "bedrock" rules of our native language are hardwired into us. To say that kids need to learn their grammar before they get to reading and writing is, to put it simply, not true.

We hope we've demonstrated that teaching some terms in the context of students' reading and writing might help them become mindful about grammatical decisions that have important consequences in their writing and reading. But our approach presumes that students are doing lots and lots of writing and reading.

Our simple answer about when to teach the terms has an important corollary: If you teach students terms when they need them and link them to their writing and reading, then the teaching of the terms can be distributed across their school years. (Of course, these "toolish" ideas can always be applied to an appreciation of, response to, or analysis of another's writing, too.) It makes no sense at all for teachers to teach the same set of terms year after year after year. We'll make the same argument in greater depth when we talk about correctness. In both cases we think this litmus test should apply: If kids aren't getting it, something must not be working. (A famous colloquial definition of insanity is to keep trying the same thing and to expect different results!) Rather than try to remedy the situation with more of the kind of teaching that has already proven to have failed, we think a different approach is called for.

Chapter 3

Thinking About Error

In Lynne Truss's very funny *Eats, Shoots & Leaves*, she urges readers to get in touch with their Inner Stickler and stand against what she sees as a rising tide of inattention to error. (Our favorite example comes in a quick aside in which she mentions that she glued an apostrophe to a stick and went to a theater marquee to demonstrate that the title of the film *Two Weeks Notice* could be easily corrected.) Our argument in this chapter is very much the opposite. We will argue that if we really want to help our students write more correctly, we need to put aside our Inner Stickler and focus our attention only on the errors that matter most. But before we do, we need to take up the question of what an error is.

Is There a Standard?

By "error," we mean a departure from Standard English (SE), though we're a bit uncomfortable with both the word *error* and the term *Standard English*. We'll start with the latter. The term *Standard English* suggests that somewhere what "The Language" is meant to be has been carved into stone. And indeed, as Schuster (2003, p. 52) points out, in 1851, Gould Brown, author of a tome entitled *Grammar of Grammars*, declared himself to be the "heaven sent standard." But the fact is that no such carved tablets exist. Standard English may be the standard by which people's language in English-speaking countries is measured, but it's important to recognize that it's simply one among many kinds of English.

Our lives would be so much the poorer if that were not the case. Jeff used to work in Maine and now that he is "from away," he misses Maine English "wicked bad" and sometimes feels "numb as a hake." As the previous sentence illustrates, although a dialect includes distinct vocabulary, it also has its own grammar and syntax. Cities or regions may have their own dialects, as might different cultural groups. One of the wonders of traveling around the country is to listen to the beauties of the various Englishes that are spoken in America.

When Jeff worked in Tasmania, Australia, he learned something about other dialects of English. During his first week of work, he asked why the curriculum director, Larry, was absent and was told, "That old bag a fruit did the frog and toad to Steak and Kidney!" Jeff quickly realized that if he thought Australians spoke the same English he did, he was badly mistaken. This is a case of "rhyming slang," which comes from the Cockney convicts who were brought to Tasmania and New South Wales. The slang is a kind of code that both disguises meanings from outsiders—for example, prison guards—and also invites others into a group of insiders. It certainly provides a colorful way of looking at the world. In the sentence above, bag a fruit → man in the suit → boss (in this case, Larry); frog and toad → hit the road → take a trip; Steak and Kidney → Sydney, where Larry had gone on a business trip. And once you figure out the rhyming slang, there are implied rhymes, so if someone asks you for a "deep sea," they are asking for a five-dollar loan: deep sea → deep sea diver → fiver.

Although dialects have their own lexicon, grammar, and syntax, they are, for the most part, understood or easily learned by speakers of other kinds of English (though some communication breakdowns may occur), for they are united by some shared principles (Schuster's [2003] "bedrock" rules). These are the rules that allow native speakers of English to quickly and easily sort the words *French the young girls four* into the phrase "the four young French girls," a phrase that will be easily understood by every other native speaker of English.

> "Standard English may be the standard by which people's language in English-speaking countries is measured, but it's important to recognize that it's simply one among many kinds of English."

You'll notice in the paragraphs above that we shifted our discussion of the English language to a discussion of English dialects. We did so purposefully. From a linguistic point of view, both language and dialect refer to a rule-governed system of communication. But the words carry different weights. As one linguist put it, "A language is a dialect with an army and a navy." That is, the word *language* suggests a kind of permanence and power that's not suggested by the word *dialect*. The statement is an important one, for it provides a critical reminder that what makes a dialect a language is not its inherent superiority as a communicative system but rather the status of those who employ it.

The fact that one dialect is commonly referred to as Standard English indicates that it has a privileged position in our culture, and we'd be doing our students a disservice if we do not help them gain access to that privilege. However, the recognition that Standard English is a dialect like any other has important implications for how we should teach it, especially how we teach it to students whose home dialect is not Standard English. Before we explore those implications, we think it's worthwhile to spend time considering the controversy surrounding the Oakland Unified School District's policy on Ebonics, for that controversy reveals how misconceptions about language have politicized what we think is a commonsense pedagogical principle supported by years of research in cognitive science: It's important to build on what students already know to help them develop new knowledge.

The Furor in Oakland

In December 1996, the Oakland Unified School District adopted a resolution, which was amended in January 1997, calling for the teachers in the district to recognize that many of its African American children were coming to school speaking a dialect different from Standard English. We've included the amended resolution as Appendix A. The heart of that resolution seems to us to be the following clause:

> Be it further resolved that the Superintendent in conjunction with her staff shall immediately devise and implement the best possible academic program for the combined purposes of facilitating the acquisition and mastery of English language skills, while respecting and embracing the legitimacy and richness of the language patterns

whether they are known as "Ebonics," "African Language Systems," "Pan African Communication Behaviors," or other descriptions.

The outcry against the district was fast and furious. Wayne O'Neil (1997), a professor of linguistics in the Department of Linguistics and Philosophy at MIT, catalogued some of the hue and cry:

> So it goes with the syndicated columns, whose titles often give some of the flavor of the attack: William Raspberry's uninformed characterization of AAE [African American English]: "no right or wrong expressions, no consistent spellings or pronunciations and no discernible rules" (*Washington Post*, Dec. 26, 1996); Ellen Goodman's "A 'Language' for a Second-Class Life" (*Boston Globe*, Dec. 27, 1996); Mary McGrory accusing the Oakland Board of "legitimizing gibberish."

The critics' primary objection resides in their concern that what they see as "gibberish" has been elevated to the status of "language" and their misapprehension that Oakland planned to substitute the study of AAE for the study of Standard English. Let's take each of these in turn.

The research on African American English is clear. AAE is not a collection of random mistakes. It is just as systematic as Standard English, though it differs from Standard English in significant ways. For example, Wikipedia (http://en.wikipedia.org/wiki/African_American_Vernacular_English) begins its discussion of the formal features of AAE by noting that the invariant use of *be* is used to describe a habitual action (e.g., *He be eating rice*, meaning *he regularly/ frequently/habitually eats rice*). Second, the Oakland resolution never suggested that AAE be substituted for SE; rather, the resolution calls for educators to respect speakers of AAE and to use students' knowledge of AAE to help students develop competence in SE.

In January 1997, the Linguistic Society of America supported Oakland's resolution with the following:

> Whereas there has been a great deal of discussion in the media and among the American public about the 18 December 1996 decision of the Oakland School Board to recognize the language variety spoken by many

African American students and to take it into account in teaching Standard English, the Linguistic Society of America, as a society of scholars engaged in the scientific study of language, hereby resolves to make it known that:

1. The variety known as "Ebonics," "African American Vernacular English" (AAVE), and "Vernacular Black English" and by other names is systematic and rule-governed like all natural speech varieties. In fact, all human linguistic systems—spoken, signed, and written—are fundamentally regular. The systematic and expressive nature of the grammar and pronunciation patterns of the African American vernacular has been established by numerous scientific studies over the past thirty years. Characterizations of Ebonics as "slang," "mutant," "lazy," "defective," "ungrammatical," or "broken English" are incorrect and demeaning.

2. The distinction between "languages" and "dialects" is usually made more on social and political grounds than on purely linguistic ones. For example, different varieties of Chinese are popularly regarded as "dialects," though their speakers cannot understand each other, but speakers of Swedish and Norwegian, which are regarded as separate "languages," generally understand each other. What is important from a linguistic and educational point of view is not whether AAVE is called a "language" or a "dialect" but rather that its systematicity be recognized.

3. As affirmed in the LSA Statement of Language Rights (June 1996), there are individual and group benefits to maintaining vernacular speech varieties and there are scientific and human advantages to linguistic diversity. For those living in the United States there are also benefits in acquiring Standard English and resources should be made available to all who aspire to mastery of Standard English. The Oakland School Board's commitment to helping students master Standard English is commendable.

4. There is evidence from Sweden, the US, and other countries that speakers of other varieties can be aided in their learning of the

standard variety by pedagogical approaches which recognize the legitimacy of the other varieties of a language. From this perspective, the Oakland School Board's decision to recognize the vernacular of African American students in teaching them Standard English is linguistically and pedagogically sound.

The Linguistic Society of America's statement makes clear the reason for our discomfort with the use of the term *error*. Often, departures from Standard English are not a result of incorrect SE; instead, they represent the correct use of a different dialect. AAE is just one example. Type "dialects of American English" into a search engine and you'll be able to explore many others. The richness of those dialects provides the foundation for the National Council of Teachers of English resolution "Students' Rights to Their Own Language," passed in 1974 and reaffirmed in 2003. (Both resolutions are available at http://www.ncte.org.)

What This Means for Us as Teachers

Schuster (2003) identifies six primary ways that nonstandard dialects of English tend to differ from SE:

1. Different verb forms. The AAE use of *be* to signal habitual action is one example. Another is different forms of irregular verbs; for example, the past tense of *bring* in AAE is *brung* rather than *brought*.
2. Double negatives or comparatives, as in "He don't know nothing" or "Vanilla is more better than chocolate."
3. Differences in subject-verb agreement, as in "She go to the store."
4. Different use of pronouns, for example, using an additional pronoun as an intensifier, as in "Joe, he can really play."
5. Using an adjective form in an adverbial context, as in "He did good" or "She comes to the diner real regular."
6. Miscellaneous words and phrases such as *ain't, anyways, this here.*

Recognizing that our students may be speakers of different dialects seems to us to have profound pedagogical implications. Perhaps the most significant is in how we regard students. Too often we've seen teachers dismiss students who speak a different form of English as stupid or lazy. Doing so is, quite simply, wrong. Too often we've seen teachers constantly correct speakers of other dialects. Lisa Delpit (1997) offers a powerful argument for how stultifying that kind of correction can be. A thought experiment helps support her views. Imagine that you're in a different country after having taken just a few classes in the language of that country (or lots of classes a long time ago). Imagine that you've resolved to try to speak the language with a native speaker. Now imagine that the native speaker interrupts you at every mistake rather than trying to understand you. We know we'd quit trying pretty quickly. We suspect that most of you would, too.

Sometimes students adopt their teachers' negative perspectives. One of Michael's former colleagues spoke AAE at home because she didn't want her children to feel distant from or superior to other members of her extended family. She told Michael a story about how her elementary school daughter was doing wonderfully well in French but was failing English. When she asked her daughter about the problem, her daughter said that she just couldn't get English. Michael's colleague said something like, "Why not, honey? It's just a new language like French. You're great in French." Michael's colleague said that this little conversation caused a light to go on in her daughter's head. When she regarded SE as a new language, she knew she could learn it. Research on the value of having confidence in one's capabilities, what educational psychologists call self-efficacy, makes it clear that believing you can do something is important to actually being able to do it. If you think that you just can't speak or write correctly (and being told that you can't promotes this attitude), you'll be much less likely to invest the effort it takes to gain competence than if you believe that you can learn SE just as you've learned other languages or your own English dialect.

Recognizing the multiplicity of dialects suggests to us a number of activities that would help teachers develop students' self-efficacy while at the same time help them learn the conventions of SE. If a class is homogeneous and speaks a dialect other than SE, the class could work together to collect samples of speech and writing in the students' home dialect, infer the rules that guided their construction, and then articulate the rules of SE, paying special attention to how it is different. For example, speakers of AAE might collect the following set of sentences: "I saw the fishes." "Mens and womens got to get along better," and "Those sheeps have long wool" (examples drawn from Labov, Baker, Bullock, Ross, & Brown, 1998). By contrasting those sentences with how they would appear in SE—"I saw the fish," "Men and women have to get along," and "Those sheep have long wool"—they could come up with the following realization: "In AAE we add *s* or *es* every time we make a plural of a noun that has no descriptors. In SE some words are already plurals; you don't have to add *s* or *es*." It wouldn't be important to come up with an exhaustive list. What would be important is to help students gain the recognition that SE operates differently than does their dialect.

If the study of language becomes central to the work of the class, students could also be asked to interview people about the ways they adjust their language in different situations. Such a project could be introduced by showing an excerpt of *My Fair Lady* or any of the myriad movies in which a character has to learn a new dialect because he or she is entering a new social situation. This assignment would work equally well in a heterogeneous or a homogeneous class.

So too would creating dramatic situations that called for students to employ Standard English. For example, casting kids in the role of a newscaster for the television news and comparing what they do in that context with what they do when cast as a disc jockey would reveal a wide variety of linguistic differences and draw attention to students' tacit ability to code-switch. Such an assignment would be especially effective after a class research project on how the news is delivered. Creating short dictionaries or guides for using particular dialects in particular situations—for example, the general dialect of students at West Junior High, or of "goth girls" in particular—is another fun project that explores these issues.

> "Constant correction is not the way to go, for it breeds frustration in both teachers and students."

Another way to employ and enlarge students' linguistic understandings would be to work with them to write classroom rules for times and situations when different dialects can be used. One way to respect students' language is to talk with them about when to use it. A policy might say that students could use their home dialect in classroom discussion, but that formal presentations and writing ought to be done in "newscaster style." As we noted above, constant correction is not the way to go, for it breeds frustration in both teachers and students. Michael's daughter Catherine, a biracial 16-year-old who identifies as African American, evidenced this frustration when she complained about how some teachers always interrupt speakers of AAE. She put it this way: "You can't be telling a Chinese person his language is wrong."

Once the class has spent some time considering different dialects, students can apply their understanding to their reading of literature. Asking the class to evaluate the linguistic authenticity of texts that employ various kinds of dialects would allow them to transfer their linguistic understanding to their reading. It might be especially interesting to compare and contrast the way that a dialect is rendered by authors from the culture being portrayed with how it's used by authors from outside the culture. Is Walter Dean Myers's representation of African American characters' language more accurate than, say, Jerry Spinelli's? We've found that students can be engaged in taking up this kind of question.

Thus far in the chapter we've argued that the term *error*, as widespread as it is, is at least somewhat problematic, for what's right in one kind of English might be wrong in another. However, recognizing that Standard English is the coin of the realm in schools and virtually all other mainstream institutions obliges us to help our students master it. Our pedagogical suggestions so far can be summarized into one suggestion: make language variation the subject of study, especially if you have kids whose home dialect is not Standard English. This means respecting their home dialects as crucially important resources and creating contexts in which they have to articulate how those dialects compare with Standard English. It means talking with them about code-switching and creating situations that tap their ability to do just that. It also means helping them speak and write in Standard English.

Errors Matter, but Not Equally and Not as Much as We Think They Do

Not all departures from Standard English are a result of dialect differences. Sometimes even when students are trying to write in Standard English, even when SE is their home dialect, their papers have errors. In responding to those errors, teachers might take out their red pens and note all of them in some way. Or, overwhelmed, they might simply ignore them all. We think both approaches are misguided.

Mina Shaughnessy, someone we consider to be one of the giants of our profession, helps explain why. Shaughnessy was a teacher of basic writing at City College of New York when the city university system adopted an open admissions policy that guaranteed every city resident with a high school diploma the right to attend college. The influx of new students was dramatic, and many of those new students had different dialects and different kinds of academic preparation than the students who had attended CCNY in previous years. The new students created tremendous new demand for instruction in basic writing.

Shaughnessy (1977) discusses her approach to teaching basic writing in her brilliant and germinal *Errors and Expectations: A Guide for the Teacher of Basic Writing*. Though she wrote for college teachers, she has profoundly influenced our thinking about how to teach middle school and high school students. One of her most significant influences is paraphrased in the heading for this section. She puts it this way: "Errors count but not as much as most English teachers think."

In the first place, most errors distract readers rather than destroy meaning. When we see a sign in the grocery that says "Eight Items or Less," we still know it's the express line, as much as we might prefer "Eight Items or Fewer." Both of us have become adept at reading (when we're allowed) IM messages that are replete with deviations from conventional spellings. As heroic as one might think Lynne Truss is for carrying the stick with the apostrophe, even without it we all knew that the notice was given two weeks in advance. Even the most egregious example of mispunctuation in her book (it might be "Bob,s Pets") communicates.

Think of it: We're able to read Huck Finn's dialect and the writing of Zora Neale Hurston. In fact, we rejoice in the beauty of their vernacular. We know from our colleagues in the content areas (those who assign writing, anyway) that it's possible for someone to ignore students' errors and focus on meaning. But it's hard.

Each of us will admit to being particularly sensitive to certain errors that just give us the willies. Michael pays far too much attention to using possessives with gerunds. A sportscaster's saying "Iverson jumping out at Kobe caused the turnover" instead of "Iverson's jumping out at Kobe caused the turnover" might even lessen Michael's enthusiasm for the ensuing layup. Jeff's concern with the correct use of *good* and *well* is a joke among his friends, who misuse the terms just to irritate him: "We skied good today!" they'll taunt. But, truth be told, we realize that the willies these errors give us are a result of some idiosyncratic concern rather than a result of a breakdown in communication.

In fact, as Connors and Lunsford (1988) point out, a historical analysis demonstrates that "teachers' ideas about errors and error classification have always been absolute products of their times and cultures" (p. 399). That is, what counts as error differs from time to time and place to place. And even from person to person. Frank McCourt begins the foreword to *Eats, Shoots & Leaves* with this sentence: "If Lynne Truss were Catholic I'd nominate her for sainthood." Should there be a comma after *Catholic*? It is, after all, an introductory adverbial clause. Hmm. And what about the use of the first-person pronoun in expository prose? He begins the next paragraph as follows: "It's a book about punctuation. Punctuation, if you don't mind!" What to make of the fragment? What about the direct address to the audience, when prohibitions against using second-person pronouns are even more stringent than prohibitions against using the first-person pronouns? We wonder what Mr. McCourt would think were we to hand back his foreword with everything circled in red that we could justify circling in red. We suspect he'd feel something similar to how we felt upon receiving this manuscript marked up by our wonderful editors. He might well ignore our marks (after all, he is Frank McCourt). Or he might do as we did and negotiate revisions. Some of what was flagged, for example, careless homonym errors, we were delighted to correct. Other items seemed to us to be more a matter of opinion than a matter of necessity. The fact is that many rules aren't as hard and fast as one might think.

Sometimes what are considered errors are violations of what Schuster (2003) calls *mythrules*, that is, rules that have a foundation in an unexplainable preference of an unnamed authority rather than in any examination of the way that people actually speak and write. One of them is to avoid splitting infinitives, a rule that seems to be derived from someone's interest in making English analogous to romance languages like French, Spanish, and Latin, in which infinitives cannot be split because they are single words. But what to do with a sentence such as the following: "She seemed to seriously believe that it was all right to cut class." Where else could *seriously* go and still emphasize that her belief was a serious one? Another example of a mythrule that Schuster provides is the injunction to avoid ending a sentence with a preposition. Schuster cites

Prospero's "We are such stuff as dreams are made on" as a compelling argument against that rule. And if Shakespeare doesn't work, how about Churchill's famous dismissal of that same rule: "This is the sort of bloody nonsense up with which I will not put."

Edgar Schuster's wonderful book (2003) provides a long list of mythrules that complement his favorite writer test. He suggests that if you are uncertain whether a rule reflects real language use, just take down a book from a favorite author and read several pages. If you find the rule violated, it is almost certainly a mythrule that does not pass the test.

This notion mirrors the idea of the *correspondence concept* currently popular in cognitive science (Bereiter, 2004; Nickerson, 1985). This concept emphasizes that teachers should teach in a way that corresponds to actual expert practice. Students should be taught to read and write in ways that progressively move them toward expertise. In other words, after every lesson, activity, rule, concept, and unit, students must have something in their heads and in their capacities that more closely matches what an expert has in her head than what students had beforehand. Otherwise, we are teaching mythology, not practical knowledge. Or, to be harsher, our teaching is making our students stupider—it is moving them away from expertise. If we are not teaching students for expert understanding and expert performance, then what on earth are we teaching them for?

> "Some errors might be more a cause for celebration than concern, for errors are often a signal of growth."

Moreover, some errors might be more a cause for celebration than concern, for errors are often a signal of growth. Our daughters are all musicians, and one of the things we love to hear is when they try a piece that's a challenge for them. As they are working to meet that challenge, mistakes are inevitable. The same is true for writing. In fact, try to think of anything of any significance you have ever learned that you got right the first time, from cooking to kissing to jumping rope. We'd contend that all significant learning requires risk taking and mistake making. It also takes social support. What can you learn without models to copy and helpers to guide you? If you ever learned to kiss or cook or jump rope (or anything else), other people helped you, encouraged you, and yes, even indulged you.

The lesson is that, as teachers, we need to encourage and even reward the mistakes that are necessary to learning. For example, students who can correctly write unadorned sentences that resemble kernel sentences in sentence combining exercises should be helped (through the kind of modeling, mentoring, and monitoring we saw in the exercises at the end of Chapter 2) and applauded for trying more complex sentences even if they do produce some errors. If we don't encourage growth in this way, students will naturally return to what is easier for them, to what is rewarded, and to what is less complex and sophisticated. In fact, Jeff's students found in independent teacher research studies that the more errors they marked, the more likely students were to retreat to simpler structures.

> "The more errors [teachers mark], the more likely students [are] to retreat to simpler structures."

As students go through school, they are challenged to read and write new text structures such as factual lab reports, arguments, extended definitions, and classifications. New genres require specific knowledge of how that text type works and often bring with them new syntactic demands. As students are working to meet those demands, they are likely to make errors. For example, persuasive papers about school policies often call for students to manage complex sentences. Students who want to write against school uniforms will likely produce complex if/then sentences that they seldom produce in their day-to-day conversations.

In summary, the idea of error is often problematic because many errors aren't errors at all but are instead correct expressions from a different dialect. Moreover, even among educated speakers and writers of SE, there are differences of opinion about what constitutes an error. Some errors have questionable origins. Even when there are no differences of opinion about an error, most do not interfere with meaning. They may even be a sign of growth. In school, students should be challenged to learn and do new things, and that will require making mistakes.

That said, it would be naïve to argue that errors don't matter at all. In the first place, saying that most errors don't affect understanding indicates that some errors *do* affect understanding. Others are sufficiently distracting that they make processing the meaning of a message more difficult. Even when an error doesn't affect understanding, it might diminish the impact of a text by undercutting the authority of the writer, especially in those contexts in which the text is all the reader has to go on to get an impression of the writer—for example, in a college application or on a high-stakes writing assessment. In our next chapter we're going to consider in some detail ways to address some common errors. But before we do, we'd like to discuss what we see as a sensible model for how teachers (or better yet, *schools*) ought to address errors.

Establishing a Hierarchy of Error

An aside: Some years ago, Michael signed up for golf lessons. Michael played regularly and was scoring in the low 90s, not too good, but good enough that he could play most courses without embarrassing himself. Because he wanted to go to the next level, he signed up for a winter's worth of golf lessons. And indeed Michael did go to another level, but not the one he was aiming for: He now shoots over 100 and has given up the game.

Why? When Michael went for the lessons, the well-meaning pro tried to change everything about Michael's swing, all at once. New setup. New takeaway. New swing tempo and pattern. New finish. So much new that Michael thought so hard about all that he had to do that he couldn't do anything at all.

Likewise, Jeff loves marathon cross-country skiing. When he moved to Idaho, he joined a masters Nordic team. His coach told him that he wasn't doing anything right and that all techniques had changed since he had first learned to skate-ski more than 20 years ago. The coach taught Jeff so many new skating and poling techniques that Jeff was quickly overwhelmed. Jeff decided that he would focus on one new skating technique during his first season. The next year he focused on a more difficult skating technique. Instead of feeling overwhelmed, he felt a great deal of accomplishment, as he had mastered both. Next season, he'll undertake a new challenge. When too many errors were focused on and too many new techniques were taught, Jeff was on sensory overload. But when he concentrated on mastering only one technique before moving on, he experienced success, albeit slowly, over time, and with lots of hard work and repeated practice.

The fact is it's extremely difficult to attend to too many new things at the same time. If we note every error students make on their papers, we're doing to them just what Michael's golf teacher and Jeff's ski coach did: undermining the effectiveness of our instruction by overwhelming students with it. Because our

Getting It Right

instruction isn't effective, we're faced with the prospect of starting over every year. Sixth-grade teachers teach sentence structure, punctuation, and agreement, and a whole range of usage issues. But because students don't learn it, seventh-grade teachers do the same. And then eighth-grade teachers. And ninth. And on and on and on. (Remember Denise from the last chapter? She decided to teach one convention of correctness in her sensorium unit: commas with items in different kinds of series. Because she concentrated on one thing, almost all of her students got it and kept doing it right through the rest of the year.)

Moreover, as teachers we spend endless hours marking the errors on students' papers. If this were an effective practice, teachers in the upper grades would have fewer errors to mark, but in our experience the same kind of errors that plague students' papers in the lower grades occur in the upper grades as well. Why do we spend those hours when it seems that we have so little to show for them?

We'd like to suggest an alternative: establishing a hierarchy of errors and addressing the errors at the top of the hierarchy one at a time, allocating the time we spend on each according to the time available for the teaching of writing. That is, instead of worrying about every error in every paper, we think it makes far more sense to focus our own and our students' attention on one issue at a time. It means modeling, mentoring, and monitoring student practice until they truly understand how a language convention works and can really use it correctly, now and in the future. (Flashback again to Denise.) That hierarchy should be based on four criteria: the extent to which the error interferes with understanding, the extent to which the error undercuts the authority of the writer, the commonness of the error, and the cost (or ease) of correction. Let's take each of these in turn.

Errors That Interfere With Communication and Understanding

As much as Michael hates gerunds without the possessive or Jeff might be distressed by the misuse of *good* for *well* or overuse of the exclamation point, we have to admit that those errors distract us, rather than interfere with our understanding. On the other hand, we both have read countless student stories with multiple characters that were unclear about who was doing what because the student writer used pronouns without clear antecedents. Ambiguous pronouns create far more confusion than other errors and therefore are more worthy of our attention. Sometimes sentence fragments also cause us problems as readers. Here's one example from a student paper: "Splash. As I run through the dark alley in the night. The monster with the purple snot all over his face." What exactly was the monster doing, we wonder? What's the relationship between the monster and the running? We're just not sure. Errors that cause writers to be misunderstood are important ones to correct.

Errors That Undermine the Authority of the Writer

On occasion errors don't interfere with meaning, but they do undercut the authority of the writer, often because they mark the writer as lacking knowledge or as a speaker of a nonstandard dialect. A sentence such as "I ain't never seen such a thing before" is perfectly intelligible, yet unless the writer was evoking the dialect for some rhetorical purpose, his or her authority would be undercut. If people share William Raspberry's uninformed view that AAE has "no discernible rules," then the following sentence from the same paper that featured the monster with the purple snot will cast doubt on the writer's language ability despite the wonderful figure of speech: "The muscles in my chest feel like they're in a vice grip and somebody keep tightening it." Even those people who believe that *like* shouldn't introduce a clause will likely regard the application of an AAE rule of agreement as a more serious problem. We know that we're much more affected when an applicant to a graduate program misspells a common word in an application through what seems to be an error (e.g., "recieve") than when an application has a misspelling that's clearly a typo (e.g., "clealry"). Even errors of a similar sort might carry a different significance. Beginning a sentence with a lowercase letter or failing to capitalize "I" marks a student as a novice writer far more than mistakenly capitalizing a grade level (e.g., "Sophomore").

Commonality of Errors

When teaching middle and high school, we know that some errors will be common across papers, and some will be idiosyncratic. As for common errors, we know that our seventh- through ninth-grade students will write an occasional fragment and display subject-verb agreement problems when a prepositional phrase whose object is of a different number than the subject of the sentence is placed between the subject and the verb (e.g., "Every one of the athletes are going to the awards assembly"). These are issues worth addressing before, during, and after student writing, and we know it even before we meet our new seventh-grade students each year. It might make sense to work with colleagues to study more formally the errors students make at a given grade level. Andrea and Karen Lunsford's research (2006) on first-year college writers provides an interesting model. (See the box Twenty Most Common Errors Made by First-Year College Students.)

Some correctness issues, however, seem to us to have a different status. Here are the last three sentences of the "monster with the purple snot" paper: "The monster bites my head off. My body shakes from my nerves like a kite in the air. The only good thing is I finally get to relax . . . in heaven." At least some style manuals say that writers should use ellipsis points only to signal omitted material. (You can Google "ellipsis points" to see the range of opinions on the issue.) Perhaps a dash rather than ellipsis points would have been a better choice for the writer. However, it seems clear that their use here reflects a sophisticated attempt to delay a surprise ending. Consequently, regardless of your views on the use of ellipsis points, we think that the student's efforts should be applauded rather than critiqued. (It might make sense to work individually with this student on the rhetorical impact of different punctuation marks even as the whole class is taking up a more common issue. We'll talk more about doing this kind of individual instruction later.)

An aside: While completing his dissertation, Jeff was astonished at how his committee (including Michael) asked for almost daily revisions, some of them quite substantive. But because he was using a word processor, most of these revisions were simple additions, cuts, or pastes. He asked his committee how students had dealt with these requests prior to word processing. Wayne Otto, a giant in reading education, had this to say: "We didn't make those requests. It caused too much trouble and work. So dissertations were short and full of mistakes!"

The point: Technology is part of a shifting situation that changes the capacity of students to meet particular demands of the writing situation and might even cause or contribute to certain kinds of errors. As situations shift (including new standards and tests), the demands placed on students and the errors students make will evolve as well, and therefore so must our teaching. In many cases, these changes allow us to have different and higher expectations for student work.

Twenty Most Common Errors Made by First-Year College Students

An interesting study first conducted for *The St. Martin's Handbook* in 1986 traced the most common errors in first-year college students' writing. In other words, the study identified the kinds of errors our best students make even after completing their secondary education. This research was recently updated by Andrea A. Lunsford and Karen Lunsford (2006), who collected and analyzed first-year college students' compositions from across the country. The results demonstrate some significant shifts in what and how students write, and the kinds of errors they tend to make.

Andrea Lunsford (2006) explains:

> First, with the help of technology, spelling errors have dramatically declined. But the study also found that wrong-word errors—for example, the kind that result when a student spells "definitely" incorrectly and allows a spell-checker to change it to "defiantly"— are the new number one error. Second, new problems related to research and documentation appear in the top twenty today. In 1986, no documentation mistakes appeared in the top twenty because students were writing personal narratives or were doing close readings of a literary text. Today, students are writing research-based essays and arguments, which demand at least some use of sources—and hence a completely understandable increase in errors related to the use of those sources.
>
> Perhaps most importantly, the research points out that students today are writing longer, more complex work for their college courses (more than twice as long, on average, as essays written in 1986)— without a significant increase in the rate of error.

Cost of Correcting an Error

Finally, we think it's crucial to be mindful of the cost of correcting an error. The cost should be measured in terms of both the instructional time it takes and of

The Top Twenty

1. Wrong word—often due to acceptance of automatic word replacement by computer
2. Missing comma after an introductory element
3. Incomplete or missing documentation
4. Vague pronoun reference
5. Spelling (including homonyms)
6. Mechanical error with a quotation
7. Unnecessary comma
8. Unnecessary and missing capitalization
9. Missing word
10. Faulty sentence structure
11. Missing comma with a nonrestrictive element
12. Unnecessary shift in verb tense
13. Missing comma in a compound sentence
14. Unnecessary or missing apostrophe (including its/it's)
15. Fused (run-on) sentence
16. Comma splice
17. Lack of pronoun-antecedent agreement
18. Poorly integrated quotation
19. Unnecessary or missing hyphen
20. Sentence fragment

You can also view the original list and accompanying examples at http://bcs.bedfordstmartins.com/easywriter3e/20errors.

the effect it will have on students' confidence as writers. We've all experienced situations in which we wanted to give up, or actually did give up, because the task seemed too hard for us and success too difficult to reach. (Both of us have experienced this as writers as well as in other domains of our lives. If we, as accomplished writers, can have our confidence eroded, how much more easily can a novice writer's willingness to try new things be undermined?)

As an example, despite the fact that writers in Spanish begin interrogatory and exclamatory sentences with upside-down question and exclamation marks, respectively, it is a relatively easy matter to teach students whose first language is Spanish not to use those upside-down marks when they are writing in English. On the other hand, prepositions in Spanish are far more flexible than they are in English, and as Reid (2004) demonstrates, the reasoning guiding native English speakers' choice of prepositions is extremely nuanced. As a consequence, teaching English prepositions to speakers of Spanish is a time-intensive task. In our opinion, preposition problems are not worth addressing, at least not until students become fluent in English.

Speakers of some Asian languages typically begin writing English without using articles, and when articles appear, they often appear where they aren't needed or when another article is called for. The rules in English for determining when an article is needed and which article is needed are enormously complex. (Try this experiment: Pick a page of a newsmagazine at random and try to explain the use or omission of articles.) Moreover, rules that have been derived may not be useful. For example, Purdue University's Online Writing Lab (http://owl.english.purdue.edu/handouts/esl/eslart.html#count) explains that indefinite articles are used with countable nouns while noncountable nouns take definite articles. Knowing this rule won't be useful if nouns that are countable in English are not countable in a student's native language. Further, as Reid (1991) notes, there are very few true noncountable nouns in English. Most nouns can be countable or noncountable depending on the context. He illustrates this point by noting that while he has two boys, his wife has said to one of them, "You and Angus cannot be in the tub together; that's too much boy" (p. 89).

Prepositions and articles are little words, ones that ELL students might think they should easily master. Imagine the impact on a writer's confidence of having a teacher point out that he or she has gotten these little words all wrong.

Addressing Spelling. It's also important to consider the time cost for students who are working on an error, an idea we'll illustrate by discussing our approach to teaching spelling. When Michael taught juniors and seniors in his school's lowest track, he sometimes had students who would make several spelling mistakes in every sentence. These students typically didn't like to write very much (we wonder why!), so telling them to look up every word they didn't know how to spell didn't seem very sensible. At the least, the time the student spent looking up words would come at the expense of time that might have been spent composing. Instead Michael asked those students to circle the words they weren't sure of. He thought that if a student could identify words that might be misspelled, that student would have a chance of correcting them in contexts in which spelling correctly was very important. Michael focused his and his students' energy on those words that the student thought were spelled correctly but were in fact not. He might do things differently now, given the ubiquity of word-processing programs, but his approach still seems to us a sensible one for students with severe spelling problems who do handwritten papers.

The ethic that informed Michael's work with his weakest spellers should also inform whole-class instruction on spelling. The key is to maximize the impact of instruction while reducing the cost in time. That's why it makes little sense to us to have weekly tests on word lists that kids may or may not use. Instead, we suggest the following four-part strategy:

1. Develop a class list of commonly misused or misspelled words that might be used in the context of the current inquiry and/or writing assignment. These can be posted on word walls, on posters around the classroom, and so on.
2. Help individual students create a short personal spelling list of important words to get right. (The list would contain five to ten common words that the student has misused in the past. It could be pasted inside the student's portfolio for easy reference.)
3. Help students learn some general rules that will help them improve their spelling over time.
4. Structure group peer-editing efforts to support better spelling.

The following box (Sample Spelling Rules Sheet) is a handout that we've found useful across classes.

Sample Spelling Rules Sheet

In the final phase of proofreading/editing, use our class list of important words and your personal list of important words to get right. You should proofread your paper using the lists, have a classroom peer editor proofread using the lists, and—for the most important papers—have your adult "keeper" (an adult who volunteers to serve as your mentor) proofread your paper using the lists. Of course, it is important to spell all words correctly, but for grading purposes you will only be held accountable for those words on the two lists. Here are some general rules:

APOSTROPHES

Rule 1:

Possessive pronouns NEVER use an apostrophe! WHEN? NEVER!!! As possessive pronouns, they already show possession.

Hers, his, yours, ours, my, its; there is no such word as *its'*. OBLITERATE *its'* and substitute *its*!

Rule 2:

Action verbs NEVER use an apostrophe. Walk's, eat's, go's, say's, complain's, write's ARE ALL INCORRECT! WHEN do verbs use an apostrophe? NEVER!!!

PREFIXES

Rule 3:

The prefixes *il-*, *in-*, and *mis-* do not alter the spelling of the root word.

il + legitimate = illegitimate, mis + spelling = misspelling, in + consistent = inconsistent

SUFFIXES

Rule 4:

The suffixes *-ly* and *-ness* do not change the spelling of the root word.

real + ly = really, final + ly = finally, wet + ness = wetness, great + ness = greatness

This is true UNLESS the root word ends in *y*—in that case, change the *y* to *i* and add the suffix:

sloppy + ly = sloppily, sloppy + ness = sloppiness, heavy + ly = heavily

Rule 5:

If a root word ends in *e*, drop that final *e* before adding the suffix *-able*, *-al*, *-ed*, *-ic*, or *-ing*. (This is almost always the case; there are a few exceptions, like *manageable*.)

Getting It Right © 2007 by Michael W. Smith and Jeffrey D. Wilhelm, Scholastic Professional

love + able = lovable, love + ing = loving, fame + ed = famed, joke + ing = joking, time + ing = timing, fine + al = final, cone + ic = conic

Rule 6:

Do not drop the *e* at the end of a word before adding suffixes that begin with a consonant.
love + ly = lovely, care + ful = careful

Rule 7:

For one-syllable words that end with ONE consonant right after ONE vowel, repeat that final consonant before adding a suffix. If the word has two syllables, double the final consonant if the stress is on the second syllable.
run + ing = running, bat + ing = batting, refer + ed = referred, BUT refer + ence = reference

PLURALS
Rule 8:

When a noun ending in *y* becomes plural, or a verb ending in *y* needs an *s* ending, then check out the letter right before the *y*. If it is a vowel, just add *s*; if it is a consonant, change the *y* to *i* and add *es*.
donkey + s = donkeys, payday + s = paydays, toy + s = toys
try + s = tries, fly + s = flies, navy + s = navies, army + s = armies, anchovy +s = anchovies

Rule 9:

When a noun ends in an *o* that comes after a consonant, add *es*.
tomato + s = tomatoes, hero + s = heroes, hobo+s = hoboes

DOUBLE VOWELS
Rule 10:

Write *ei* when the sound is a long /a/, as in eight, neighbor, sleigh, weight—or a long /i/, as in height.

Rule 11:

Write *ie* when the sound is a long /e/, as in field, shield, piece, wield, yield, EXCEPT after *c*, as in receive, deceive.

Rule 12:

Believe your spell-checker unless you have a strong reason not to.

Getting It Right © 2007 by Michael W. Smith and Jeffrey D. Wilhelm, Scholastic Professional

Addressing Homonyms. The importance of thinking about the cost of teaching correctness in terms of instructional time becomes clear when you examine the many homonym/word-confusion errors that students make. When Jeff taught tenth and eleventh grade, he followed the example of his tenth-grade teacher James Blaser and tracked the mistakes his students made. He found 89 such problems (see Appendix B). Imagine trying to teach all of them! You'd have no time to do anything else.

But the truth is, some of them didn't occur all that often and some of them just aren't that important. Our suggestion, therefore, is to provide students with a resource like the one in Appendix B that they can consult as they write and to explicitly teach the entire class only a few of them. Here is our top 10 list, mistakes that we've encountered often and that seem to us to undercut a writer's authority:

1. advice – advise
2. affect – effect
3. accept – except
4. principal – principle
5. than – then
6. their – there – they're
7. to – too – two
8. wear – we're – were – where
9. who's – whose
10. your – you're

Your list might be different, but we suspect it would have many of the same items. We'd recommend that you focus on teaching only five or so during a class and that teachers get together to decide which classes would be taught which words (there's much more on working together to address errors in the next section of the chapter). Another way to address homonym usage is to assign kids who make errors to create a cartoon like the example at right, or another visual reminder of the distinctions.

Jeremy Heinrich

Sharing the Burden

If we're going to spend more time focusing on fewer errors, we'll have to share the responsibility for teaching correctness with our colleagues. In the section that follows we provide several models of how to do so.

Focused Attention Across a Grade

Thinking about the extent to which an error interferes with understanding or undercuts a writer's authority, how common the error is, and the cost of correcting it will provide a good starting point for developing a hierarchy of error. We recommend the entire department work together to develop hierarchies and to decide which errors should be addressed in which grades. For example, teachers in a middle school might decide that sixth-grade teachers will focus on fragments and run-ons, end marks, and the most common homonym confusions, while the seventh-grade teachers add on agreement and apostrophes and the eighth-grade teachers add on the syntactic (e.g., parallelism) and mechanical (e.g., punctuating introductory clauses) issues associated with increasingly complex sentences.

It doesn't matter *how* a school divides responsibility across grades as long as it does so. This kind of distribution of effort allows teachers to teach what they do teach deeply and students to have the opportunities, time, and assistance to master and understand what is taught. If teachers can focus their instruction and attention on a small and discrete set of mechanical issues, they'll be better able to attend to the content and style of their students' writing in addition to its correctness. And focusing instruction on a few important areas at a time increases the probability of success.

A Proposal for Dividing Genre Assignments and Errors by Grade

As we've argued, it is important to divide up responsibilities for teaching both particular language conventions/correctness issues and genres. If we don't, teachers will feel compelled to do too much and nothing will get enough focus to be adequately practiced and mastered.

Particular genres or text structures (as we saw with the sensorium in Chapter 2) require particular syntactic structures and correctness conventions, so, as best you can, it is important to teach students the tools they need for the genre they are studying.

Again, what's important is not how you divide the list of genres and related correctness issues, but that you divide responsibilities so that no teacher has to do too much. And there aren't hard-and-fast rules on exactly which structures and correctness issues to teach with a particular genre. However, it *is* important to teach a structure that can be usefully applied in the context of an assignment and to focus on only one or two structures or correctness issues at a time. Though there are many effective ways to divide the material across various grades, we will model our thinking for one way of doing it here.

We suggest focusing at each grade level on one type of personal narrative, one type of fictional narrative, and one kind of expository structure that usefully leads to or is itself a form of argument. As brain researcher Barbara Hardy (1977) maintains, "narrative is the primary mode of mind" and therefore is the best way to get kids writing and working on various composition strategies. We like the idea of moving from personal narratives (for which students can mine personal experience for material, so we know they'll have something to say) to more conventional narratives that make up the basic structures of literature. But we agree with Jerome Bruner (1987), who maintains that there are both narrative and paradigmatic ways of thinking and composing meaning and that each has a particular power. In both academic disciplines and democratic societies, argument is the most powerful of the paradigmatic structures, so we also focus on developing students' capacity to argue.

This does not mean that students at each grade level will write only the three genre pieces, but it does mean they will get repeated practice with each of them over the course of the year. As students practice each genre, they could also focus on the related syntactic structures and correctness issues. These will also get repeated attention and practice from various angles.

As we consider the sequencing of these genres across grades, we apply basic principles of sequencing instruction that we have written about elsewhere (Smith & Hillocks, 1988; Wilhelm, 2001, 2003; Wilhelm et al., 2001).

These general principles for sequencing can be consolidated as follows:

> Move from:
> Self to other (writer-based to reader-based)
> Close to home (personally lived experience) to farther from home
>   (from the known to the new)

Concrete to abstract

Visual and visually supported to nonvisual

Short texts to longer texts

Simple to complex

Basic structures to more elaborated structures

Personal Narratives. Our plan for sequencing personal narratives and associated conventions looks like this:

Grade 5: Autobiography of discrete experience/s (fragments)

Grade 6: Themed autobiography that explores one aspect of the writer's life, such as a literacy autobiography (verb tense)

Grade 7: Memoir (run-ons/comma splice errors)

Grade 8: Multimedia profile of self (comparatives)

Grade 9: Personality profile of classmate (quotations)

Grade 10: Process description/how-to of an area of expertise—e.g., kayak rolling, fly tying, quilting, making a pie or peanut butter sandwich (punctuating transitions)

Grade 11: Personal essay/soapbox topic (punctuating complex sentences)

Grade 12: College application essay (punctuating parentheticals and other clarifiers)

To briefly summarize our thinking: Various strands of research (e.g., Bereiter & Scardamalia, 1987) indicate that students have an almost limitless supply of personal experiences to draw on as writers. So writing autobiographies of discrete experiences is an easy place to start to help students write more fluently. Themed autobiographies require writers to relate several discrete experiences in some facet of their lives and so put greater demands on writers than writing about a single experience. Both of these kinds of writing are excellent preparation for writing a memoir in which diverse experiences are used to illustrate a pattern or patterns. If students have saved their earlier writing, they can use that writing as data to discern patterns and then develop those patterns more fully by adding additional experiences. Moving to a multimedia profile of the self takes the memoir in the direction of multimodal historical scholarship, as students incorporate photographs, video clips, drawings, and hyperlinks. In grade 9, we shift from self to other as students profile each other, requiring interviewing, checking sources, and entering another's perspective. In grade 10, students write about an area of personal expertise in such a way that a neophyte audience can learn from and understand it, adding the dimension of the reader to their prose. A personal essay that strives to convince the reader to adopt the author's point of view on an issue can extend the sphere of writing from concrete experience to intellectual abstraction. And in grade 12, the most important personal writing many students undertake is the college application essay. For those not planning to attend college, this might be an encouragement to consider doing so as well as a chance to write a final piece exemplifying one's self during the high school years.

Again, this list privileges particular kinds of personal writing and could certainly be ordered differently. For each, we have matched a correctness issue that would certainly be applied and rewarded in that kind of writing. For example, verb tense is not likely to be much of an issue in a personal experience that focuses on a single event, but it is sure to be an issue when a writer starts to juggle multiple events and to discuss them. These are focused choices, not an exhaustive list. We're not claiming that the correctness issues we identified are the only ones that could be taught. We are saying, however, that some kind of focus is crucial if our kids are to get what we're teaching them.

Fictional Narratives. In addition to personal narratives, which are always close to home and grounded in student experience, we want students to experience more challenging narratives that operate according to the conventional rules of literature. For fictional narratives, the list might look like this:

> Grade 5: Fables (homonym use)
> Grade 6: Folktales (clarity in pronoun reference, pronoun-
>   antecedent agreement)
> Grade 7: Myths of explanation (compound sentences and com-
>   pound verbs)
> Grade 8: Hero quests (punctuating participles, absolutes, and other
>   descriptors)
> Grade 9: Coming-of-age stories (punctuating dialogue)

Grade 10: Ironic monologues/stories with unreliable narrators
(using punctuation to communicate dialect differences)

Grade 11: Satires/parodies (using stylistic fragments)

Grade 12: Multi-episode stories of students' choosing (hyphens,
dashes, and the rhetoric of punctuation)

Our sequence is based both on common curricular demands and on the increasing complexity of the texts. Fables, for instance, are short and have a directly stated main idea in the form of a moral. Folktales are typically a bit longer and communicate a cultural value more implicitly. Myths contain deep truths that are typically expressed metaphorically, so they are more abstract than are folktales. The hero quest is a tale of the human journey and psychic development, so it is more complex than a myth. Coming-of-age stories will be well known by students but are less conventional than hero quests. Monologues rely on the reader's ability to understand and assess the reliability of the speaker, placing a new demand on reader and writer. Satires and parodies require background knowledge of the satirized subject and build on the ability, developed with unreliably narrated monologues, to imply a meaning beyond the literal. A short story, not confined to a particular genre, seems the freest and therefore the hardest form to tackle.

Again, applicable correctness issues are matched to each genre. For example, folktales are likely to have several characters, so the ability to use pronouns clearly is key. Hero quests often have passages of physical description, so it makes sense to work with students on using participles and other descriptive techniques as they write them.

Expository/Argumentative Writing. As we've already argued, expository and particularly argumentative discourse is central to knowledge making and the hands-on work of academic disciplines and democratic citizenship. So we will emphasize argumentation in our third set of writing emphases.

Grade 5: Fact-based reports/summaries/paraphrases (subject-
predicate agreement)

Grade 6: Persuasion (apostrophes)

Grade 7: Review writing of movies and books (capitalization,
punctuation of titles)

Grade 8: Argument of judgment (punctuation of introductory elements)

Grade 9: Argument of policy (parallelism)

Grade 10: Argument of extended definition (punctuation of restrictive and nonrestrictive clauses)

Grade 11: Argument of classification/I-search (consolidation issues)

Grade 12: Controlled research paper/extended research paper (punctuation of citations)

Our thinking here is that all argument is based on establishing and using certain kinds of evidence in particular ways. In grade 5, students gain experience by writing fact-based reports, summaries, and paraphrases. In grade 6, students engage in persuasion, which Robert Scholes defines as "not nice nor fair," an attempt to "subdue thought by appealing to emotion" and "ignoring alternatives" (1981, p. 87). He considers persuasion something to be produced when needed, but more important, to be understood and constantly defended against. It is inferior to argument, but sometimes a part of arguments: "Where persuasion seeks to put the mind to sleep so that an appeal to emotion will be effective, argumentation aims at an unemotional appeal to reason" (p. 102). It seems to us that persuasion can be a fun precursor to argument because it allows students lots of language play with connotation.

Reviews are a simple argument familiar to students from television and the Internet. By starting with movies and other popular culture events like concerts, kids can be engaged in reading and writing reviews and then easily proceed to book reviews and the like. By grade 8, students should be ready to bolster their opinions in new ways, with evidence from beyond their personal experience. This lays the foundation for arguments of policy that take place in a wider arena, that are for a more distant and more sophisticated audience, and that require more profound disciplinary knowledge. Extended definitions of abstract ideas are a particular kind of argument often pursued in mathematics and the sciences. Likewise, arguments of classification are important in the content areas and depend upon the ability to define and give examples of "classes" of data. Experience with these analytical techniques can be used in the I-search paper (Macrorie, 1988), in which students explore a topic of personal interest, and then in grade 12 with a controlled research paper (e.g., one that requires students to use sources provided by the teacher) and then a more extended research paper using a variety of sources found by the student.

Once again we've tried to identify correctness issues that are likely to arise for each kind of writing. For example, summaries are likely to contain many simple sentences, a perfect place to focus on subject-predicate agreement. Reviews, of course, contain lots of titles and names. What better time to focus on capitalization? Definitions require students to consider the essential features of what they are defining; therefore, they're a good place to tackle the difference between restrictive and nonrestrictive clauses.

Similar lists can be drawn up for, say, poetry or multimedia projects. But this is the point: By following a sequence, each year students will get repeated and focused practice with three different genres and three or more associated correctness issues. Students and teachers can be confident both that students have mastered the text structures and conventions emphasized during the year and that they have a strong background to carry forward to the tasks at the next grade level.

Attention to Individual Issues

Within this framework, specific attention can be paid to individual students as well. If individual students are having particular problems that aren't common to the class, you can address them one at a time. Michael kept a recipe box on his desk full of three-by-five cards on which he indicated the particular issues he was working on with each individual student (in addition to whatever the focus was for the whole class). Jeff keeps a sheet on the inside of each student's port-folio that indicates both the class and individual goals for that semester.

Some goals came from us. Paragraphing might be an individual goal for those students who tend to write longer pieces. Punctuating dialogue might be an individual goal for some story writers. An individual goal for other students might be straightening out *to/too/two* or another homonym error. In addition, there was always a place on our cards or lists for concerns that our students articulated about their own writing: "When do you use hyphens in a word?" We think it is important to help focus students' energy and attention on important issues, but also to help them to identify important issues for themselves.

It's essential to give topics the time and attention that real learning requires. We are reminded of the old joke about the student in the accelerated class who says, "We learn so fast, I've forgotten everything already." Our impulse is always the opposite: to spend the time that is necessary to address our focus and to stick with it until kids achieve mastery. Only then will we move on.

Ways of Focusing a Class and Individual Students on Targeted Errors

To conclude this chapter, we'll review some ideas and show some examples of how we help students to attend to a very focused and clearly identified set of errors or language conventions.

Double-Entry Criteria/Goal Sheets

On the inside cover of student portfolios we like for our students to keep a set of goals for their writing. One side of the sheet lists the shared classroom goals (such as those in our proposal for sharing the load). The other side is for a few individual student goals. Here's an example.

Language Usage Goals

Class Goals

Use studied homonyms correctly

Use commas with introductions

Personal Goals

Spell words from personal list correctly

Increase sentence variety

Use commas correctly

We also like to use a check sheet, analytic scale, or rubric of primary traits that students use throughout their composing. This document becomes a cover sheet that is signed by the author and two peer editors before it is turned in.

Of course, we primarily focus on content and genre features. Since mechanical correctness is an important but somewhat separate issue, we provide dual grades: one for content and structure, and another for mechanical correctness in language use.

This tactic provides several advantages for us and for our students. First, we can emphasize content and genre features, but not at the expense of mechanical correctness. Second, we can weight the two grades in different ways. For instance, for a struggling student, we can make the mechanical grade less important without ignoring it entirely. Third, students can see how they are improving in each area.

Following are two examples of dual grading sheets that provide guidance in responding to student writing. The second one is designed for two peer reviewers.

Dual Grade Sheet

Please fill out all of the boldface items and attach this sheet to your final paper. I'll add my assessment to yours.

Writer's name: _____

Assignment: _____

Purpose: _____

Audience: _____

	Points S/T		Points S/T
Content criteria:		**Format criteria:**	
1.		1.	
2.		2.	
3.		3.	

Total for content: Total for format features:

Student comments: **Student comments:**

Teacher comments: Teacher comments:

Setting the Task Before Us!

Student goals:

Teacher goals for student:

Getting It Right © 2007 by Michael W. Smith and Jeffrey D. Wilhelm, Scholastic Professional

Dual Grade Sheet With Peer Review

Fill out the top portion and attach this sheet to your paper. Your peer reviewers and I will fill out the rest.

Writer's name: _____

Assignment: _____

Class goals for content:

Personal goals for content/something to try:

Class goal for mechanics:

Personal goals for mechanics/something to try:

_____

Content comment Peer reviewer 1:	Mechanics comment Peer reviewer 1:
Content comment Peer reviewer 2:	Mechanics comment Peer reviewer 2:
Content comment Teacher:	Mechanics comment Teacher:
Something to try next time:	Something to try next time:
Grade for content:	Grade for mechanics:
Peer reviewer signature:	Peer reviewer signature:
_____	_____

Getting It Right © 2007 by Michael W. Smith and Jeffrey D. Wilhelm, Scholastic Professional

An advantage of personal spelling and usage goal lists is that students can add concerns of their own. Eventually, students can articulate all of their own critical standards and create their own checklists, which is, of course, what they must do in their own lives.

Muy Graves Errors

Another technique we like to use is to post a list of *muy graves* (very serious) errors in our classroom. This list can incorporate the entire class list or just the most important items. It can also include all the skills the students are accountable for and have been working on over the course of the year. (It has always struck us as unfair for teachers to mark errors or issues that they have never taught students to address.) The list can also include errors that are an automatic deduction on the state writing assessment or that students vote as especially irritating and in need of eradication.

After we've generated our list of errors, students create charts that give proofreading cues and models addressing the errors. See the following *Muy Graves* Error List that takes up the issue of run-ons.

Focused Peer Editing With Criteria Sheets

There are several premises underlying these tools. Most important, they require the students to do the work. The model, mentor, and monitor sequence requires gradually releasing responsibility to students so they can become independent users of what we are teaching. (We're reminded of John Goodlad's [1984] assertion that school is a place where young people go to watch old people work! Jeff often jokes with his middle schoolers that *he* has already passed seventh grade. Now it is their turn!) If we want our students to become problem solvers, proofreaders, and engaged readers and writers who can apply their own critical standards, then we have to provide them with both the help and the opportunity to do so in the classroom.

Second, we believe that students need to be taught what we want them to learn, and we define teaching as providing focused help and supported practice over time with seminal strategies. Each tool provides that focused help and practice. Third, we believe that once a paper is turned in, the learning is done.

Muy Graves Error List! Horrors! Horrors! Horrors!

Name:

Class Goal: Correcting Run-ons   Assignment:

ERROR/EDITOR'S MARK	PROOFREADING CLUE	FIXING THE ERROR	MODEL
Run-on Put *RO* in the margin next to the run-on sentence.	*And, so, but, or, for, nor, yet* used in a long sentence. Scan for these words, then see if the sentence contains too many complete thoughts that could stand independently in different sentences.	Place a comma in front of the linking word to show that each clause has its own subject and verb. *or* Divide a super-long sentence into separate sentences.	Ida really wanted to see the movie but she was too late and she had no money for popcorn. *Change to:* Ida really wanted to see the movie, but she was too late, and she had no money for popcorn. *Or:* Ida really wanted to see the movie, but she was too late. Also, she had no money for popcorn.
Run-on Put *RO* in the margin next to the run-on sentence.	*However, moreover, in addition, nonetheless,* and other logical linkers. Scan for these words, then see if the sentence contains two complete thoughts that could stand independently.	Place a semicolon in front of the logical linker and a comma after the logical linker.	Fiona had trouble concentrating therefore she could not proofread very well. *Change to:* Fiona had trouble concentrating; therefore, she could not proofread very well.
Comma splice (a particular kind of run-on) Put *CS* in the margin next to the comma splice.	Scan for a comma in the middle of the sentence without a conjunction before the second half. Check each side, and if both can be turned into a question that can be answered yes or no, you have a comma splice! E.g., My run was almost over, I was so tired. Was your run almost over? Yes. Were you so tired? Yes = dreaded comma splice.	Three options: Replace the comma with a period or a semicolon. Put a short conjunction before the comma. Use a logical linker in place of the comma.	Jasmine was relieved when she started skiing, she had the right wax on. Was Jasmine relieved? Yes. Did she have the right wax on? Yes. Comma splice? Yes. *Change to:* Jasmine was relieved when she started skiing. She had the right wax on. *Or:* Jasmine was relieved when she started skiing because she had the right wax on.
Personal Goals			

Getting It Right © 2007 by Michael W. Smith and Jeffrey D. Wilhelm, Scholastic Professional. Original idea from Elyse Eidman-Aadahl, National Writing Project.

All the interminable hours of grading and circling errors have very little or negative payoff for student learning. That's why the tools focus on avoiding problems or fixing them rather than on noting their existence. Finally, we believe that writers often are motivated by the need to communicate with an audience. And we have learned the hard way that our students are often much more motivated by the response of their peers and other folks out in the world (parents, keepers, coaches) than they are by the response of teachers. For all these reasons, we believe that it is important to help students to help each other. This is why we want student writing groups and peer editors to review papers for a few specific features and errors before they are turned in to us.

An additional advantage of focusing on a short list of mechanical issues is that all students will know the issues, will have had practice applying the rules, and therefore should be able to assist one another. It seems to us that a lot of peer revision and editing is not of much help because the peer editor may not know enough or be critical enough to assist the writer. Using a hierarchy of error to focus the class on a few key issues over the course of the year circumvents this problem. As a result, when papers come to us, they are in better shape, and we are in a position to highlight strengths and one or two possibilities to work on. Grading becomes quicker, easier, more useful, and more fulfilling.

On all criteria sheets, we typically have two lines for the signatures of peer editors. Sometimes we grade peer editors on the quality of their advice or give them a percentage of the grade of papers they edited.

Peer Reviewer/Writing Group Guides

In keeping with our mantras of helping kids to do their own work and allowing them to articulate some of their own standards, we help our students articulate their own standards for peer editing and group work in general.

Quite simply, early in the year we ask them to individually write down what a good group looks like, sounds like, and feels like. They then share their ideas in groups and we create a composite class list, which becomes our set of guidelines. (Sometimes we also ask students to describe what a good group *doesn't* look, sound, or feel like.) Typically, every class we have ever worked with comes up with similar guidelines, much like the following:

A Good Writing or Peer Editing Group

Looks like: People paying attention, leaning in, nodding, smiling.

Sounds like: People being supportive and nice, saying, "I like how you did X"; encouraging, praising, asking useful questions about the criteria: "What are you trying to do here?" "I hear you saying . . ."; asking, "I wonder what would happen if . . ."; making suggestions in helpful ways.

Feels like: Warm and fuzzy, like you are listened to, like people are trying to help you do your own work, not do their work.

General Guides for Peer Editing Work

Though you can use sheets that list specific criteria, like the dual grading sheet shown earlier, sometimes general sheets can guide a peer editor's work. Following are two good ones we use that help peer editors internalize powerful ways of responding to and assisting one another's writing.

Jeff learned the following technique at the Maryland Writing Project from Jenny Killgallon (coauthor with her husband of several sentence combining books of note) and has adapted it in various ways over the years. (See the Word Processing Peer Revision/Editing Sheet.) The idea is that when writing on a word processor, it is easy to make five basic revision moves that mirror computer commands: **Keep** a section or sentence that is really good, **Add** something like an example or more specifics, **Move** a sentence or section to somewhere else, **Delete** a section or sentence that doesn't work, **Change** a sentence or construction so that it is more effective. Likewise, the sheet can be used for mechanics by using these commands: Keep to identify and praise risk taking or a usage goal met, Delete or Change for mistakes.

You can also adapt the use of the sheet in various ways; for example, if you want your students to practice praising each other, then require them to give two Keep commands and explanations before giving other commands.

The sheets provide a section to explain the peer editing suggestion, and a space for the author to accept, adapt, or reject the suggestion. We emphasize that the composition is the work of the author and that therefore she has final authority. However, we do ask that students explain their reasons when they reject a peer editor's advice.

General Peer Response and Editing Sheet

PURPOSE/SO WHAT?

1. What was the purpose of this assignment? For what personal or real-world reason did the author compose this?

CONTENT/WHAT?

2. How well did the author meet her purpose? How do you know?

3. Summarize the content and point in a "telegram" of one to three sentences, the shorter the better!

AUDIENCE/WHO?

4. Who is the audience for this piece and how is this audience accommodated and addressed?

QUALITY/HOW?

5. Praise—what I liked best:

6. Question—what I would like clarified or would like to know more about:

7. Considerations/suggestions—I wonder what would happen if . . .

MECHANICS/USAGE

8. Class usage goals for this assignment:

How well did the author meet these goals? Please mark the margin with a + where the goal was met and with a – where the goal still needs to be addressed. Do not mark the error itself; let the author find and correct it!

9. Personal usage goals for this assignment:

How well did the author meet these goals? Please mark the margin with a + where the goal was met and with a – where the goal still needs to be addressed. Do not mark the error itself; let the author find and correct it!

Getting It Right © 2007 by Michael W. Smith and Jeffrey D. Wilhelm, Scholastic Professional

Word Processing Peer Revision/Editing Sheet

Provide the author you are helping through peer editing with at least six pieces of advice by using the commands Keep/Add/Move/Delete/Change. Depending on the revision or editing phase, you might be focusing on content and structure or on mechanical issues. Start with a Keep, but use no more than two Keep commands.

Keep/Add/Move/Delete/Change Command _____ Reason: Author chooses to ___Accept　　___Adapt　　___Reject Reason for adaptation or rejection:	**Keep/Add/Move/Delete/Change** Command _____ Reason: Author chooses to ___Accept　　___Adapt　　___Reject Reason for adaptation or rejection:
Keep/Add/Move/Delete/Change Command _____ Reason: Author chooses to ___Accept　　___Adapt　　___Reject Reason for adaptation or rejection:	**Keep/Add/Move/Delete/Change** Command _____ Reason: Author chooses to ___Accept　　___Adapt　　___Reject Reason for adaptation or rejection:
Keep/Add/Move/Delete/Change Command _____ Reason: Author chooses to ___Accept　　___Adapt　　___Reject Reason for adaptation or rejection:	**Keep/Add/Move/Delete/Change** Command _____ Reason: Author chooses to ___Accept　　___Adapt　　___Reject Reason for adaptation or rejection:

Portfolio Entry Cover Sheet

To help students become conscious of their progress and capable of tracking it, we ask students to attach a cover sheet for submissions to their portfolio. The following Portfolio Submission Report provides a sample. Jeff learned this technique from Kathy Egawa of the National Council of Teachers of English.

This kind of cover sheet can be amended to focus on punctuation or the language convention currently being studied, by using questions such as these:

1. One way I used (semicolons, commas with introductory phrases, etc.) was:

2. One place where I tried something new with punctuation or sentence construction was:

At the end of each semester, we like for students to write a cover letter for their portfolio in which they explain how they have improved as writers, using evidence and examples from their portfolio, including their use of different language conventions.

The important thing is to help students to become more competent, self-aware, and confident as writers. Giving students a chance to see signs of improvement and growth toward a small and clear set of attainable goals can help this to happen.

Portfolio Submission Report

Name: _____ Date: _____

Title of work sample: _____

The following piece is entered into my portfolio because

_____ it demonstrates mastery of this skill, construction, or technique:

_____ it shows risk taking and an attempt to try this new skill, construction, or technique:

_____ it shows growth and progress when I compare it with:

_____ it shows these specific stages and processes that I used to complete the work:

What I like best about this piece is:

An important thing I learned from doing this piece is:

Something I want to remember and do next time is:

Friend/keeper notes:

Peer editor notes:

Teacher notes:

Chapter 4

Cherchez le Cause

A couple of stories to start. Michael and his wife, Karen, moved to Madison, Wisconsin, from Chicago not long after they were married. When Karen's parents planned their first visit, Karen thought it would be nice to set up a golf outing. Both of her parents are avid and very good golfers. Karen doesn't golf, but she said she'd walk along. We've already mentioned what the pro did to Michael's swing, but Michael agreed to go along for the sake of family unity. Along about the fifth hole, Michael was coming out of the woods yet again to join his playing companions as they walked the fairway to the green. Karen walked up to Michael and whispered out of the corner of her mouth, "If you'd just hit it in the fairway, we could all walk together." "Why didn't I think of that?" Michael thought to himself.

The first time Jeff's wife, Peggy, watched him ply his kayak in a playhole along the Penobscot River, she asked: "Why do you flip upside down so much? Why don't you just surf on the wave instead of rolling over all the time?" "Ah," Jeff thought, "that's how it works! The wave actually wants me to ride it and doesn't want me to be knocked off! It should be simple!"

If it were only that easy, our wives' efforts to improve us would have been far more successful. But it's not. Michael hit the ball in the woods not because he was antisocial but because he has big problems with his golf swing. Jeff kept getting dangled upside down because waves constantly change their shape, and his reactions are obviously just not that fast!

We hope that you chuckled along with our stories, but we hope you see a serious point in them as well. What's true for Michael's golfing and Jeff's kayaking is true for our students' writing as well. When we circle misspelled or misused words or bracket problematic constructions, we're doing to our students just what our wives did to us. Our chapter title, an allusion to the advice "Look for the woman" (given to countless detectives investigating a man's bad behavior), provides what we think is a far more productive approach. If errors happen for a reason, you can't fix them simply by noting their existence. You have to find and then address the cause. We think that's such an important idea it's worth repeating: *If errors happen for a reason, you can't fix them simply by noting their existence.*

Some Common Causes of Error

Throughout our years as middle and high school classroom teachers and into our work with student teachers, we've studied patterns of student errors in grammar and usage, developed theories about their origin, and refined our understandings. In this chapter we identify some likely causes of common errors and provide a variety of strategies for addressing each of them.

Dialect or Language Interference

In our last chapter we discussed at some length the fact that many errors are a function of differences between the student's home language or dialect and Standard English (SE). We also explained why speakers of African American English (AAE) seem to be particularly at risk for being dismissed as illiterate because of their language. AAE is close enough to Standard English that it's often heard as a series of mistakes rather than as a consistent system. We described some activities we'd do to raise students' attention both to the systematicity of AAE and to the differences between AAE and SE, so we won't belabor the point here. But we do think it's worth noting that if dialect or language interference is the cause of an error, that error will not be easily fixed.

In many cases it will make sense to wait a while before you try to address language interference issues. As students become more familiar with Standard English, they'll pick up some of the tacit understandings native speakers have about the language. But those understandings will come slowly. If you have African American students who speak AAE, waiting will probably not be enough. After all, they have been exposed to SE through the media and through their schooling. If you want to teach them to add an *s* to the end of a verb to make it agree with a singular subject, one of the major differences between AAE and SE, you have work to do.

After you've done enough language study so students see the difference between AAE (or other dialects) and SE on subject-verb agreement, and after you've looked at enough examples of SE to help students derive the rule that because the -s form of the verb is singular while the -s form of the noun is plural, the two -s forms can't be combined as a subject and its predicate (see Shaughnessy, 1977, p. 146), it's time for plenty of practice. (This is worth repeating too: To achieve mastery at anything, *students need lots and lots of practice over time and in a meaningful context, such as their own writing.*) You might begin with subjects that have conventional plurals and then move to subjects that don't. It would be a great idea to collect sentences from students' own writing to help them see the mistakes they make as well as why and how to fix them. Here are some examples we drew from stories students wrote in which they described a chase as vividly as possible:

> The pit bull look/looks like he just finished eating a child with no help.
> My body feel/feels like 1,000 watts of high voltage energy.
> The man scream/screams, "I'll get you."

Because these "chase" stories were told by a first-person narrator who was typically running from a solitary pursuer, they were an excellent vehicle to help students recognize not to use the -s form when the subject is singular.

Even this kind of extended practice isn't enough, for the agreement rule is very complex. The -s form isn't used with the main verb of a singular subject if the verb has a helping verb. The -s form is not used with an infinitive. So it's important to do a little bit at a time, to be patient, and to provide students with plenty of opportunities to develop their understanding, as much of it as possible through their own writing. That means both using their writing to generate examples and to create situations in which they have to produce the target structures in their own writing.

Other languages have different sources of interference. Fu (2003) delineates major differences between Chinese and SE. Chinese verbs, for example, don't have tenses. Adverbs are used to indicate past, present, or future. Chinese verbs don't change with the subject. Nouns don't have a plural form—they remain the same regardless of number; a number or a quantity adjective is used instead. Pronouns don't have different cases. Word-order rules are different as well. Rolon (2004) identifies a number of variations between SE and the Spanish spoken by the Puerto Rican community college students he studied, among them the use of the present tense in past narrations, the formation of progressive tenses, and the use of the double negative.

We could go on, but the purpose of this book isn't to offer a comprehensive set of contrastive analyses. Besides, we propose that every teacher needs to be a teacher-researcher of her students' learning performances and her own teaching. A little bit of research is all it takes to find analyses of different languages that your students speak. In many schools, one or two languages dominate, so it would be worthwhile for departments to work together to look for patterns in the errors of students of a particular linguistic background.

> "Every teacher needs to be a teacher-researcher of her students' learning performances and her own teaching."

Or you can ask your students to do some writing in their home language, translate it word for word, and then contrast their translations with SE. Doing so would be especially useful in school contexts in which students have a wide variety of home languages. In our experience, students and even parents are often eager to work as coresearchers on such a project.

Though there are differences across languages, we think that there are principles that ought to inform the approach one should take in helping students whose home language isn't SE. If the cause of an error is language interference, addressing it will be difficult and will take time. *It will surely make sense to tackle only one or two errors at a time.* As we argued in the last chapter, we think it makes sense to develop a hierarchy of errors. When it comes to language interference, we think it's especially important to consider the cost of correcting an error. For example, it makes sense to wait on the errors that require the most nuanced understanding of English, such as articles or prepositions. They take a tremendous amount of time to address, and even then you may not be successful. Once you've identified an error or two that are simpler to address, we think it makes sense to begin with a contrastive analysis, especially if you have many students in your class with the same linguistic background. Then you have to give students lots and lots of practice recognizing the error, correcting it, and *producing* the target structures.

Consolidation Errors

Academic writing often requires students to produce structures that they seldom use in conversation. They are called on to embed quotes and to provide citations or attribute these quotes in some sentences. (This can be especially challenging for cultures with longstanding traditions of using other people's ideas or words through "sampling" or "voice blending," in which the listener is supposed to know the original text, and not citing it is an act of respect. This practice has long been a part of African American culture.) They are called upon to contrast their arguments with what an opponent might say. (In some cultures, arguing or taking issue with an authority is considered disrespectful.) They are asked to include many more descriptive details than they tend to do in speech (because the people you are talking to may be able to make many assumptions from their prior knowledge of you and your experience that a reader cannot). In short, they are asked to manage a kind of complexity that they don't have to manage in their speech.

If the cause of such errors is inexperience and unfamiliarity, the solution is practice. As we've seen, one of the great virtues of sentence combining is that it provides extended practice in managing complexity. What follows is what a sentence that might appear in a persuasive paper on school uniforms looks like when it's unpacked into sentence combining kernels:

School uniforms reduce decisions.
The decisions are about what to wear.
The decisions are faced every morning.
School uniforms reduce costs.

The costs are of clothing.

Many students hate school uniforms.

They say school uniforms are boring.

They say school uniforms reduce individuality.

These kernels can be combined in many ways. Here are some possibilities:

> School uniforms reduce decisions about what to wear in the morning;
> they are also cheaper, but uniforms are boring and don't show
> individuality, so many students hate them.

> Although school uniforms reduce decisions about what to wear in the
> morning and are cheaper, many students hate them because they
> are boring and reduce individuality.

> Many students hate uniforms because they are boring and reduce
> individuality, but they also cost less and reduce decisions about
> what to wear every morning.

> School uniforms are cheap and reduce decisions about what to wear
> in the morning, but many students hate them, they are boring
> and reduce individuality.

These examples show that sentence combining can provide an opportunity to discuss correctness, in this case the comma splice in the fourth sentence. But the examples also reveal that there is much more to consolidation than correctness. Talking about the relative merits of each of these sentences would also involve considerations of the impact of starting a sentence with one's point or an opponent's point. Discussion could also focus on the importance of streamlining one's sentences and whether it even makes sense to write a sentence as long as any of these. Extended work with sentence combining serves as a common project that provides both efficient practice in managing long sentences and the opportunity to examine the impact of the choices different writers make to communicate the same ideas. When designing sentence combining activities, keep these suggestions in mind:

> ▸ Relate the exercise to the writing assignment at hand so there is
> a real context for immediate use.

- ▸ Use examples from student drafts, if possible.
- ▸ Discuss different choices and the effects of each.
- ▸ Develop tools that help students remember and apply what they have learned.
- ▸ Have students create their own sentence combining models from their own papers.
- ▸ Have students use/highlight/justify some of the choices they've studied in the writing assignment at hand.

Not Acting Like a Writer

Another common cause of error is that students often don't behave like experienced writers. One significant way that students' behavior differs from that of experienced writers is that they often don't reread what they have written. For example, each of us has taught units on descriptive writing in which we encouraged students to add descriptive detail. Here's a passage from a seventh-grade student's description of her living room:

> If the window is raised you can hear the wind's sweet lullaby. Which would make you happy and peaceful.

We imagine what was running through the writer's mind when she wrote the passage might have been something like this:

> Okay, let me write a sound detail: "If the window is raised you can hear the wind's sweet lullaby." That's good. Oh wait, he always asks for details and we just did that lesson on describing what you feel, so let me add something: "Which would make you happy and peaceful."

In addition to relative clauses like this one, we would often get participial phrases, as in "When I finally stopped running, I saw the dog. Grinning from ear to ear." Or sometimes we'd get adverbial clauses: "It was pitch black outside. Even though it was supposed to be daylight." And sometimes we'd get the second half of a compound predicate: "The man stared at me with a wicked smile. And then started to run right at me."

Our diagnosis of the cause of the problem stems in part from our elimination of other possible causes. Since the majority of the sentences our students write and speak are complete sentences, we know they have a good sense of what a sentence is. This means that doing grammar exercise after grammar exercise in which they underline the subject and predicate can't help solve the problem. After all, if you construe the fragments in the above examples with the sentence that precedes them, all of them are complete. (Another problem that contributes to fragmenting is that spoken speech is often fragmented. For instance, if we ask one of our daughters why she didn't put away the dishes after dinner, she might reply, "Because I have too much homework to do!")

Instead of having students underline subjects and predicates, we encourage them to read as they're writing by modeling how we do just that when we compose (see Jeff's work on teacher think-alouds in Wilhelm, 2001). We also create a situation in which students have to reread by not letting them turn in papers until they have read their paper out loud to one or two of their classmates. To avoid students' reading across punctuation so that the fragments sound as though they are part of the sentence that precedes them, we ask students to read backward, sentence by sentence, beginning with the last sentence and continuing to the first.

In their teacher research, Jeff's students found that the editing process was most successful when kids received two kinds of assistance: (1) general support in *how* to proofread and (2) specific support in using particular proofreading cues for the kinds of serious errors—ones that interfered with communication—they actually tended to make.

One way to provide specific support for fragment finding is to help the class create two sets of words: "promise words" and "beware words." Promise words are those that promise sentences will have two parts: relative pronouns (which, who, and so on) and subordinating conjunctions (after, although, and so on). Beware words are those that cause problems for more than one writer in a class. Participles were at the top of our beware list. We had students keep lists of both sets of words in their writing notebooks and encouraged them to reread what they had written when they used them in their writing. At the very least, we

---

Tips for Proofreading for Fragments

▶ Reread your paper backwards, sentence by sentence.

▶ Read your paper aloud to other students with a double pause after each period or end stop.

▶ Look for *-ing* words used as verbs and make sure they are attached to a helping verb like *is* or *was*. If not, add the helping word or change the verb. Check other beware words.

▶ Look for words that promise a sentence will have two parts (e.g., words such as *which*, *who*, and *whose* or *after*, *although*, and *because*) and make sure the sentence does indeed have two parts.

---

thought they'd attend to the words when they heard themselves read them aloud before turning in their papers.

If students are not reading their work as writers do, using analytic scales and help sheets can encourage them to do so. Here's an analytic scale and a help sheet (see page 99) that we've used in a unit on descriptive writing.

Analytic Scales for Descriptive Writing

5. You describe a variety of details. None of the details seems out of place. The description is specific, accurate, and creative. When I read the paper, I feel I really understand what you have experienced.

4. You describe details in this paper. None of the details seems out of place. The details are specific and accurate. It would help me understand the experience more fully if you used a greater variety of detail. Or you could use more creative descriptions, especially more figures of speech.

3. You use some details in this description, but I have difficulty understanding what you experienced. Combining some of these suggestions will improve your paper: describing more specific details, writing more creative descriptions, making sure all the details stick to the central point, or using different kinds of details.

2. It's hard to understand what you experienced. You could make your description less confusing by observing more carefully. If you observe more carefully, it should be easy to include more details and to describe them more specifically and creatively.
1. You don't really have a beginning attempt at describing what you have experienced. It will take effort to improve this paper. You should remember to use your senses to make careful observations. If you use your senses, there should be lots to write about.

As Michael has pointed out (Smith, 1991), students in school are engaged in developing their sense of competent activity and staking their identity through their developing competence. The psychoanalyst Erik Erikson (1963) called this the developmental stage of industry versus inferiority and identified the central psychosocial conflict of this stage as identity versus role confusion. The risk is that students who do not see themselves as developing competence in a particular activity are almost certain to reject it because it makes them feel inferior and threatens their identity.

Analytic scales foreground students' competence even as they help students work toward even greater competence. They make the criteria for competence clear and show that writers develop along a continuum over time. During peer response, the scales and help sheets give all parties a common set of criteria and tools for assessing students' progress. This minimizes confusion and insecurity. By using the analytic scales, we can avoid the lack of clarity and objectivity of many traditional assessment models, which tend to have diffuse criteria that range over many different features and rely on a teacher's subjective general impressions instead of clearly articulated standards (Hillocks, 1986). By using the help sheet, we can make sure that students can support the way they used the scales.

Remember, one common cause of errors is that students don't reread their work; therefore our work with scales is designed to promote rereading. When writers reread, they do so with an eye to improving their work, so we encourage rereading by promoting revision. One way we do that is by modeling how we revise a section of text, then by having the whole class work together to use the same strategies to revise a common paper, one that students have given a low

Help Sheet

(to be filled out by peer reviewers)

Name of writer: _____

Name of helper: _____

Content:

If you gave the paper a 5:

    List what senses the writer appealed to.

    Underline four or five details that were especially effective.

If you gave the paper a 4:

    Point out two places where you were hoping for more detail. (Use arrows in the margin.)

    List a kind of sense detail that the author didn't use but could have.

If you gave the paper a 3:

    Mark any confusing details with a *C*.

    Point out two places where you were hoping for more detail. (Use asterisks in the margin.)

    List a kind of sense detail that the author didn't use but could have.

If you gave the paper a 2:

    Mark any confusing details with a *C*.

    Point out two places where you were hoping for more detail.

    List a kind of sense detail that the author didn't use but could have.

    Underline at least one description that could be more specific.

If you gave the paper a 1:

    List four or five details that the author could have included.

Sign here if the writer read his/her paper out loud from the last sentence to the first:

_____

Correctness:

Underline the *-ing* words used as verbs and make sure they have a helper such as *is* or *was*.

Underline all the "promise" words. Make sure that each one is in a two-part sentence.

Getting It Right © 2007 by Michael W. Smith and Jeffrey D. Wilhelm, Scholastic Professional

rating when they developed their scales or when we introduced the scale to them. We work as a class to make the changes that would improve the rating of the paper. Then students work in small groups or pairs to revise an additional paper, with our guidance and help, as needed. In this way, we apprentice them toward independent revision of their own work. (Notice the use of modeling, mentoring, and monitoring students to independence through the gradual release of responsibility, Wilhelm, 2007).

In the words of Haneda and Wells (2000), we try to encourage students to regard writing as an *improvable object*. If students regard their writing as improvable, it's far more likely that they'll begin to read it with a critical eye. And if they have been supported and assisted in learning how to make improvements with scales and help sheets, then it's even more likely that they will do it well.

Our work with scales and help sheets is informed by the following principles:

- ▶ Proceed from doing work for the students (modeling), to doing it with them (mentoring), to having them do it by themselves (monitoring).
- ▶ Provide multiple modes and measures to support and assess learning.
- ▶ Provide time and support for practice, practice, practice.
- ▶ Foreground and celebrate students' capacity to improve and their control over making improvements.

Phonology/Inexperience With Print

Many errors students make come from their attempts to use words and phrases in their writing exactly as they hear them. When Michael began teaching, he was taken aback by the number of his students who used *nexstore* as an adjective describing a person who lives nearby. It took him a while to realize that what students meant was *next door*. But upon reflection, their mistake made sense. It's very hard to articulate all of the consonants in *next door*. Students who don't read much won't have seen the phrase *next door* used as a description. If they can't draw on what they've seen to produce writing, then they have to draw on what they've heard. Likewise, Jeff's students often wrote *Ossum!* in their compositions, which confused Jeff until he realized this was the word *awesome*.

A classic example of students' writing what they hear is using *of* instead of *'ve* as in *should of* instead of *should've*. So too are misspellings like *walken* for *walking*, which come as a consequence of speakers' tendencies not to articulate the endings of some words.

The good news is that errors resulting from phonology and students' inexperience with print are far easier to remedy than those that stem from language interference. Sometimes simply explaining to students their confusion and what accounts for it will be enough. It was for eliminating *nexstore* and *ossum*. Sometimes it will take more than that. In our experience students needed more work to avoid writing *could of, would of,* and *should of*. If a substantial portion of a class is having that difficulty, it makes sense to add *of* to students' list of beware words or indicate on their personal help sheets that they should check each use of *could, would,* and *should*.

Another useful strategy for raising students' attention to the ways that speech transmutes words is to stage short improvised dramas in which students are cast, say, as aristocrats or opera singers who take care to fully pronounce all of the letters in the endings of words, perhaps interacting with common people whom they affect not to understand. Or students could perform sketches in which confusion results from the misspelling (on a poster, announcement, letter, or advertisement) or the mispronunciation of particular words. These dramas are especially effective in a short series of lessons on dialogue in which different characters pronounce the same words in different ways. Here are some ideas for this type of assignment.

Model Assignment: Improvised Speech Drama

▸ Create a short script in which conflict and confusion are caused by different kinds of pronunciation and speech patterns.

▸ Choose some characters who speak differently and come from different social classes and backgrounds—for example, your grandmother, a Hell's Angel motorcyclist, a cheerleader, an honor student, a former boyfriend or girlfriend, a philosophy professor at the local university.

▸ Choose a place and situation—for example, Thanksgiving dinner and your sister has just started dating the motorcyclist and the philosophy professor objects to eating animals. Or you are stuck on an elevator with a former boy/girlfriend, and his/her new squeeze.

▸ Write some dialogue and see what happens!

Here's a student example featuring Grandma, a Rap Star, and a Valley Girl at Thanksgiving dinner.

RAP STAR: Yo yo, G-ma, slip me some poes.
GRANDMA: Pardon?
VALLEY GIRL: Duh, grandma. He's all like, "Pass the poes," and
    you, like, don't get it. He totally wants the potatoes.
GRANDMA: Then he should have asked that in the first place.
RAP STAR: Hey, you dissin' me?
GRANDMA: He wants a dish of what?
VALLEY GIRL: Ugh! This is so totally uncool.
GRANDMA: Oh, dear, are the potatoes too hot?

Paragraphing

Rather than just taking a red pencil to a kid's paper and marking paragraphing errors, we suggest that you see the cause as inexperience with print. It's important to recognize the cause, and if you decide to address it, address it fully. As Schuster (2003) points out, paragraphing is an art, not a science. Students who write what he calls "obese" or "anorectic" paragraphs may not have enough experience reading texts to have developed a feel for when authors make paragraph breaks. We know that we're guided both by the structure of the writing we're doing and by the way it looks on a page when we're making paragraphing decisions. As experienced readers and writers, we've developed both a readerly and writerly sense of when to end a paragraph.

If students are having difficulty making paragraphing decisions, it will likely help to encourage them to develop both of these senses. You can do so by handing out copies of a couple of articles and asking them to discuss which ones look the most inviting. You can ask them to try to articulate the reasoning behind the paragraphing decisions the authors of those articles made. Or you can hand out a published article or a student paper that has been broken into single-sentence paragraphs and ask the class to combine these into larger paragraphs in various ways. You might give them a longer piece that is not paragraphed and ask groups to decide where to insert paragraph breaks and have the class discuss their decision. Schuster suggests giving students examples of both "obese" and "anorectic" paragraphs and asking students to evaluate them. In all of these activities you're increasing students' thoughtful attention to print and in so doing addressing the cause of a problem that many of them might share.

Lindemann (2001) points out that paragraphs make promises to readers. Paragraphs raise readers' expectations for some kind of shift or change in emphasis, a new example or reason, a counterpoint, a new topic or subdivision of the topic, a new speaker, and so forth. Writers use paragraphs to chunk the page into smaller units because readers like to deal with ideas in manageable bits.

Paragraphs can also be manipulated for effect. For example, one-sentence paragraphs draw special attention to themselves. Short paragraphs tell us that an idea needs to be considered separately or savored in some way.

Relevant to our discussion of mythrules, Lindemann points out that in various studies of professional writing, anywhere from 50 to 90 percent of paragraphs don't possess a topic sentence. And real writers do not consciously begin paragraphs with such sentences. Sentences, paragraphs, and longer works are about seeking and showing different kinds of patterns and relationships among various ideas. Once again, conventional wisdom can lead us away from real writing.

Another excellent exercise for teaching paragraphing along with sequencing and structuring the relationship of ideas within a text is the mystery pot activity. To create a mystery pot, you need to find a tightly constructed short text (*Reader's Digest*, for example, is a great source of such texts), type it into separate single sentences, and then cut the sentences into separate strips. Students are asked to put the sentences into the best order and to decide where to insert paragraph breaks.

Even as students are learning about paragraphing, they are also learning about different text structures. Understanding how to structure text is an important tool for many different kinds of intellectual and disciplinary work.

The activity also teaches about transitions and other cohesive devices. Students have to organize the sentences by recognizing connections between them. Making and communicating connections is the essence of knowledge building and understanding (see, for example, Perkins, 1986; Wilhelm, 2007).

The exercise in the following box is an example of a mystery pot activity that Jeff has used to explore narrative text in his "Who will survive?" unit. It comes from a World War II–era *Reader's Digest*.

Lack of Confidence

Another common cause of errors is students' lack of confidence. Shaughnessy (1977) discusses why students' lack of confidence can magnify

---

Narrative Mystery Pot

Arrange the following sentences into their proper original order. Pay attention to how each sentence connects to the previous one and to the evolving effect of the whole. **Tip: Circle elements that cue you to where the sentence is positioned in the text relative to other sentences. Draw arrows from particular words to their antecedents.** When you are done, provide a title and a callout, and then paragraph the sentences in a way that makes sense to you. For extra credit, provide an illustration that could go with the story.

1. Hunger, thirst, and the Caribbean sun began to madden and kill them.
2. The torpedo struck at dusk.
3. From a hospital in the Canal Zone last week came one of the grisliest tales from the war.
4. He was lying there waiting for death when his lifeboat nuzzled into a small steamer.
5. Another, in demented fury before he died, tossed the one bucket of recently caught rainwater overboard.
6. In launching, the lifeboat turned over, and Kelly and his shipmates hid under it when the sub cut loose with deck guns.
7. It was told by a haggard, wan-eyed bearded sailor, who looked like a man of 50.
8. His open-boat voyage had lasted 21 days.

---

their difficulties with Standard English. Because they are uncertain and don't want to assert themselves, they may start sentences with empty fillers. (A memorable example from one of Michael's ninth graders: "I think though I am probably wrong that . . ."). They may also avoid asserting themselves by not using active verbs or by adding many qualifiers. The extra verbiage often makes their syntax more difficult to manage. "There are in my opinion many reasons why most students basically should decide to join extracurricular activities" raises many more issues than does "Students benefit from extracurricular activities."

---

9. After that it was all bad.

10. When things quieted down, they righted the boat and bailed it out, found that they had 11 cans of condensed milk, some hardtack and chocolate, a compass and a small dictionary with a map of the Western Hemisphere.

11. They ate seaweed and some of them drank seawater.

12. On the stern of the tanker, Kelly and ten shipmates struggled frantically with a lifeboat.

13. First, somebody stole the milk and drank it.

14. By the third week only Kelly and another mess boy were left.

15. The cook, with $163 in his pockets, stepped casually over the bulwarks, remarking, "I'm just going across the street to get some pineapples."

16. He was a mess boy named Robert Emmett Kelly, aged 17, sole survivor of a middle-sized tanker that a Nazi sub spotted somewhere in the Caribbean.

17. Without milk, the men were afraid to eat the hardtack and chocolate.

18. Another shipmate ate a jellyfish and jumped screaming over the side.

19. "After that," he said, "I laid down and tried to make myself comfortable, hoping that I could die without any more trouble."

20. The cargo of petroleum was ablaze in an instant.

21. When his sidekick gave up, Kelly waited 36 hours before he tossed him overboard to make sure he was really dead.

If students' difficulty writing correctly in SE stems in part from a lack of confidence, then teachers must address that lack of confidence in their teaching. We argued previously that scales can increase students' confidence by providing clear evaluation criteria and the opportunity to meet these criteria. Monahan (2001) took what we think is another promising approach. She set up a dramatic classroom exercise in which her sixth-grade students took on the role of investigators trying to determine what caused the unexpected loss of product at a soft drink manufacturing plant. The details of the case required students to grapple with scientific concepts that she had taught them, such as condensation and changes in states of matter. The scenario encouraged them to advocate confidently for the position of the characters they were playing. She demonstrated that her students wrote more confidently voiced (maybe even too confidently voiced) essays as they tried on their new identities.

Research on situated learning (Brown, Collins, & Duguid, 1989) demonstrates that not only do learners require a meaningful situation to contextualize and coproduce their learning, but also that the lack of a context leads to mislearning and misconceptualization. The drama provides a powerful context for motivating and supporting learning.

It also provides roles and identities to try out. As Gee (2003) points out, all learning is a form of identity work. Learning, in fact, can be construed as the apprenticeship of learners into communities of practice—the possibility of being, behaving, thinking, and performing like a real practitioner. Becoming a better writer (or mathematician or social studies student) requires the learner to be able to imagine and rehearse being a particular and new kind of person, a kind of person who would like to write and could be good at it (or who could practice ethics, mathematical thinking for engineering, etc.). Contrast this with what our informant Buda told us in our study of the literate lives of boys both in and out of school (Smith & Wilhelm, 2002): "School teaches you how you are dumb, not how you are smart." By encouraging students to try on the roles of experts, we're demonstrating that we think they're smart.

"Becoming a better writer . . . requires the learner to be able to imagine and rehearse being a particular and new kind of person."

Lack of Confidence With New Genre Structures

When Jeff's student teachers studied their own students' compositional problems, a major cause was their students' unfamiliarity and lack of confidence with the new text structures they were being asked to write. We have already discussed (Chapter 3) how each text structure presents its own particular challenges in terms of syntactic structures at the sentence level. However, as students write in new genres, particularly expository ones, they experience a more global problem: linking sentences with previous sentences, coherently connecting paragraphs, sensibly developing and justifying complex ideas, and providing an overall structure to their writing that meets both the conventional demands of classification, definition, argument, and so on as well as the navigational needs of readers.

We've also already discussed our discomfort with the term *error*, and this stretches the idea of error a bit further. But our point is that "getting it right" in composing doesn't just apply to word and sentence-level issues. As our students move from writing narratives of personal experience (as we noted in the last chapter, Barbara Hardy [1977] calls narrative the primary mode of mind and our preferred way of knowing and organizing experience) to much more complex, less familiar, and more conventional structures like subverted narratives (with unreliable narrators, changed time order, irony, etc.) or expository structures, they will need specific assistance with global issues of textual construction. Furthermore, these larger structures impact local-level structures, including the use of transitions, antecedents, internal references, and repetition of ideas and structures. Specific assistance with these elements will help students both as readers and writers.

Genre-Specific Mystery Pots

We've been arguing that correctness is not just a matter of local-level correctness. Global issues like audience and purpose, and particularly issues of text type or genre construction, are also important. That's because the text itself, in its entirety, provides a context and focus for composing. "Getting it right" in terms of genre conventions is important to student confidence for both generating the material to write (content) and shaping that material (form and genre), at both the sentence level (e.g., particular sentence structures) and text level (e.g., using appropriate transitions necessary to coherence, clarity, and navigating the text as a whole).

One powerful form of assistance for promoting confidence in this domain is using text-structure mystery pots. To start, find or compose a short text that models a fairly pure example of classification, extended definition, argument, directions, process descriptions, dramatic script, or whatever other genre you are teaching at the moment. Such a text, called a concentrated sample because it is short, compacted, and accessible, provides a good way to introduce a text structure. (Please note: Text structures rarely exist in a pure form and are typically embedded as substructures in a superstructure. For example, arguments often embed classification, extended definition, or narrative. Extended definitions typically embed description and compare-and-contrast structures. But for introductory purposes, a clear, simple, short, and tight example of the structure is most accessible for students.)

To proceed with confidence in both their reading and writing, students will have to become attuned not only to the conventions of the text structure and come to understand how such structures work, but also to the transitional elements that tie the various parts of the structure together. Doing so will tune them in to the navigational devices authors use to tie their text together and guide a reader's experience and thinking.

Even so, there will be variations in the students' reconstruction, each providing different emphases, nuances, or meaning to the final text. Students will need to consider what is important to establish first in a particular kind of text, what relationship can be established with the audience and how to do this, how to exert one's own voice and identify oneself within the structure, how to order points for maximum effect, how to emphasize the central message and its nuances, how to conclude to bring things home, and so forth. These explicit understandings will lead to metacognitive awareness and confidence that will promote sentence and text generation. It is powerful for students to see that the same textual elements can be structured or transitioned in different ways with different communicative effects. Activities such as mystery pot foreground the agency and decision-making power of the writer, help students be more wide-awake to text construction both as readers and writers, widen the writer's (and reader's) repertoire, provide more competence and control, and therefore increase motivation for writing. Such activities also debunk and provide an alternative to formulaic ways of teaching writing that bore students and move them away from true understanding and expertise with composition.

We've found that beginning with short mystery pots helps students get a sense of different text structures and the use of transitional and developmental elements. You can then proceed to longer texts. Students can do these in groups, which provide a gamelike atmosphere, and justify their conclusions to the whole class, highlighting the use of key words and transitions. The following mystery pots introduce text structure and coherence.

Put the following sentences into the correct order and be able to tell the class how you figured it out. You can use circles and arrows to show sentence-to-sentence connections and coherence.

Chronological narrative
_____ a. The game went into the sudden-death overtime period.
_____ b. In the second half, the teams went all out and took many chances.
_____ c. Fiona made a cartwheel kick and the ball shot past the goalie for the win.
_____ d. Ida, though totally exhausted, slid to the ball and passed it to Fiona.
_____ e. At the end of regulation, the game was still 0–0.
_____ f. In the first half, both teams played very cautiously.

Directions
_____ a. Be sure to beat the batter for two full minutes.
_____ b. Find a recipe for the cake you want to bake.
_____ c. Put the batter in a pan and bake for 40 minutes.
_____ d. Then add the milk and eggs.
_____ e. Check to be sure it is done by inserting a toothpick and making sure it comes out clean.
_____ f. Blend the shortening and sugar before you add any other ingredients.

We've used a similar activity to acquaint students with the genre of cause and effect. We cut the following sentences into strips and then asked students to put them in a logical order.

Cause and Effect

The most important event in the history of our country was the Revolutionary War.

The winning of independence from England had several kinds of permanent effects for the American colonies.

First, there was no more inherited privilege, but a system of merit.

As an example, inherited titles were done away with.

Land granted by the king to loyalists was made public.

Next, civil rights were broadened.

For example, voter rights were expanded.

Based on these voter rights, a federal republic with a central government and separate state governments was established.

To protect the individual citizen and his rights, the federal government was divided into three parts with balancing powers: the judicial, the legislative, and the executive branch.

The judicial branch concerned itself with interpreting and enacting the law, the legislative with making law, and the executive with the day-to-day management of government.

Because Americans were so protective of their independence, no important decision could be made without the agreement of all three branches.

As a result, individual freedoms were protected from centralized authority.

Third, the power of the British Empire was shown to be vulnerable.

In this way, the American Revolution served as an inspiration and model to later revolutionary movements around the world.

Identifying and Using Transitions. In their research, Jeff's student teachers found that disorganization and missing or inappropriate transitions were often the result of students' unfamiliarity with text structures they were using.

A good way to introduce a type of text or genre is to ask students to read several short examples. They can rank these in order of effectiveness and articulate the purpose, a definition, and criteria for this type of text, as with the introduction to the sensorium project. They can get an overall sense of the structure that will guide their reading and writing of this genre. They can look for and identify formal features, such as the kinds of transitions and linking elements the authors use to provide coherence, show how ideas relate, and create a sense of development, continuity, and connection for the reader. Students can circle these features while reading, draw arrows from the linking word back to the idea it refers to in a previous sentence or paragraph, and then come up with lists of transitions, which they can put on a poster for reference and use in their own writing and revision. All of this promotes confidence and competence. You can also have them attend to the punctuation conventions writers use to signal these transitions. By learning the conventions of a new text structure, they gain the confidence they'll need to produce it on their own.

Through their reading of short examples, our students come up with transition lists like the following.

For narration: storytelling, process descriptions and reports, chronology

after	during	next	third
afterwards	finally	now	until
as	first	second	when
at the same time	later	simultaneously	while
before	meanwhile	then	

For description: descriptions, sensoriums and place descriptions, settings

above	beyond	nearby	overhead
across from	farther	next to	opposite
also	further	on my left/right	there
at the bottom/top	here	on the horizon	to the left/right
before me	in front	on top of	
below	in the distance	over	

For adding ideas, elaborating, exemplifying: argument, analysis

again	finally	i.e.	similarly
also	first . . . second . . .	in addition	such
another	third	likewise	such as
at the same time	for example	moreover	too again
besides	for instance	one example of . . .	viz.
e.g.	furthermore	another example	

For showing cause and effect: argument, cause-and-effect papers, research papers

accordingly	at this point	for	since . . . then
as a result	because	hence	therefore
at last	consequently	if . . . then	thus

For comparing and contrasting: comparison/contrast, pro/con, problem/ solution, extended definition, classification

although	in contrast	on the one hand	otherwise
but	nevertheless	. . . on the	still
however		other hand	yet

For concluding expository texts:

in summary	in conclusion

Writing From Models. Giving students models to write from, whether composed by the teacher, other students, or professional writers, provides what are called "mentor texts" (see, e.g., Anderson, 2005). These models provide a map, a template, a set of implicit directions, a scaffold and safety net for student writers. Using such texts also helps students read like writers and write like readers.

When Jeff's cadre of preservice teachers looked at the use of various kinds of interventions for helping kids to write and write more correctly, they found that modeling, sentence combining, and inductive language-use activities effectively built student confidence, engagement, and achievement on dimensions of correctness, coherence, generation of ideas, sentence variety, and genre knowledge.

They also found that models were hugely helpful in overcoming writer's block, particularly with reluctant writers. Models of unfamiliar sentence, paragraph, and text structures encouraged students to try these structures in their own writing and helped them correctly manage the complexity of the structures when they did so.

The models you use can help students do a variety of work. Models build confidence through familiarity, and they can foreground particular sentence structures, formal devices for text construction, or text structure conventions, depending on your instructional purpose at the time.

Writing from models of particular sentence structures can do the same kind of work as sentence combining or inductive exercises. Here is an example from Samuel Johnson's letter to Lord Chesterton, who had refused to help Johnson until Johnson had already become successful on his own (from Scholes, 1981):

> The notice with which you have been pleased to take of my labors,
> Had it been early,
> Had been kind;
> But it has been delayed
> Till I am indifferent, and cannot enjoy it;
> Till I am solitary, and cannot impart it;
> Till I am known, and do not want it.

Imitating this sentence can give students practice in parallel structure as well as the use of the semicolon to balance elements between and within clauses. Students can discuss how meaning is compressed and thought concentrated by such a structure, as well as considering how many elements are not enough, too much, and just right.

Students can follow the model to write ironic thank-you letters of their own, or letters to and from characters they are reading about, or to describe cafeteria meals or other unpleasant experiences. For example:

> The dessert Will and Brad made us last Friday night,
> Had it been sweet and delicious,
> Had been appreciated;
> But I felt compelled to dump it down the disposal,
> Because it was bitter, and I could not swallow it;
> Because it was rubbery and lumpy, and I could not chew it;

Because it looked and smelled like cow patties, and I could not
stand to look at it or smell it.

Writing from models of specific kinds of paragraph structures can help students
think just a bit more globally about crafting their texts. In Chapter 2 we discussed
creating parallel structure in a sentence. Here is one that uses the same device for a
whole paragraph (based on an idea from Shepherd & MacDonald, 1975):

Tobymorry was one of those bright, handsome, no-nonsense, "I'll do what
I want and you can't stop me" cats who is a treasure to find. He wasn't a
fighter, but other animals always seemed to make way for him. He could
outrun any other animal on the farm or neighborhood, although stalking
gave him more satisfaction. He was a great adventurer, and he loved to
hunt mice and ride in a bike basket. He could be as regal and ferocious as
a lion, but he knew how to purr, curl on your lap, and be gentle.

Students can read the text, even analyze its structure if you like, and then write
the same kind of paragraph using the same kind of parallel structure to describe a
favorite pet, a friend, or a person or character they are currently studying or reading
about. It often helps if you spontaneously compose a short piece based on the model
to give the students an idea of how it is done. They will also get to see your fits and
starts, your corrections and backtracking. They'll see that writing is a messy business
that always involves some struggle. Because the model provides a scaffold for students' efforts, it helps them develop their confidence as writers. For example:

Mr. Wilhelm is one of those curmudgeonly, mercurial, "Let's put the
pedal to the metal and never stop" kinds of teachers who is an absolute
whirlwind you will never forget. He wasn't much of a lecturer, but
when he talked the students seemed to listen. He could argue about
almost anything, but helping his students to argue was his goal. He
was a great risk taker, and he loved to try new assignment ideas and do
dramas with the class. He could be as tough and unyielding as a
mahogany bench, but he knew how to encourage, praise, and make
students feel good about what they had achieved.

It is also important to model the process of composing and structuring generic text structures that are new to the students, and to have students write from these models.

This can easily be done with short poems. The poet Kenneth Koch made a career out of helping students to read and write poetry by following the models of great poets. If you choose a poem wisely, you can teach several things at once: punctuation, parody, and poetry reading and writing.

Here's an example Jeff likes to use from Stephen Crane.

> **A Man Said to the Universe**
> A man said to the universe:
> Sir, I exist!
> "However," said the universe,
> "That fact has not created in me
>   any sense of obligation."

When students write from this model—by having someone address an inanimate object, idea, or force and then having it reply, perhaps in an ironic or deprecating way—they might come to appreciate irony at the same time that they learn how to designate speakers and speech through the use of the colon, commas, and quotations.

Teaching Text Structure

Let's look at how to teach text structure by focusing on a particular one, classification. This will serve as a model for the process you can use to teach any text structure.

Classification is an essential tool in math, the physical and social sciences, and the humanities. Accurate and precise classification is the basis of biological studies and many of our most enduring and explanatory theories about life. It is essential to all forms of inquiry, giving the researcher a way to chunk data and see new patterns and relationships (see Wilhelm, 2007). For that matter, classification and pattern seeking are essential to good reading (seeing repeated patterns and the complex implied relationships among them). One of the hallmarks of good writing in the content areas is the capacity to organize data through classification, which in turn allows the writer to both perceive and express new insights. Yet it is rarely taught explicitly, causing difficulties for students in their reading and writing.

To introduce both the tool of classification and its text structure, you can provide students with a quick model:

Leonard Hooper, a lifelong resident of Down East Maine, had this to say: "You can divide residents of Maine into three groups: the Mainers or natives, the transplants, and the 'folks from away.'"

By looking closely at each group, we can come to a more precise understanding of each.

1. The natives, a.k.a. "Mainers" (pronounced "Maine-Uhs" by the locals): These are residents who were born in Maine and have lived in Maine their whole lives. These people typically work in the timber, fishery, or other outdoor-oriented industry, or in the tourism or service sector.

2. The transplants: These are people who migrated to Maine from somewhere else and have stayed for at least 10, if not 20 years. This longevity has demonstrated their love of Maine and has led to their acceptance by Mainers. They typically came to Maine for a new way of life or a kind of employment tied to Maine in some way. They interact positively with Mainers and share their concerns.

3. Folks from away: These are part-time residents, a.k.a. summer people, who have homes or "camps" in Maine. They come and go, or are construed to be in Maine for a short stay. They are not perceived as being committed to Maine values of local control, love of nature, and willingness to put up with hardship. Mainers and transplants interact with these folks out of necessity or for economic benefit, but in general resent them as outsiders taking advantage of Maine without substantively contributing to the culture.

This short example demonstrates how a social scientist will translate casual local classifications and "cover terms" (those used by real people) into a more formal, systematic, and complete set of groupings.

A great follow-up is to create a classification system of the student body. This can be done in writing, but it might also be done visually. Students can also write classifications on other kinds of topics with which they are very familiar, such as types of homework, cafeteria food, curricular activities, sports, breakfast cereals, junk foods, television shows, and movies. (See the box Cursory Classification Introduction.) In fact, you can frontload their classification writing by first having them list all the examples of a category that they can think of. They can then work to chunk and classify the list. We often start with groceries and grocery stores, so that students can begin to address classification problems with familiar material.

We have students create issue trees that reflect their classifications of familiar material. This is a powerful tool for discovering and representing the relationships between various classes and examples. This can also be done in the form of a power outline (with each number reflecting an increasing level of specificity). These in turn can become the outlines for writing an explanation of the classification. Here's an example of the form a basic issue tree might take, followed by a power outline based on school activities.

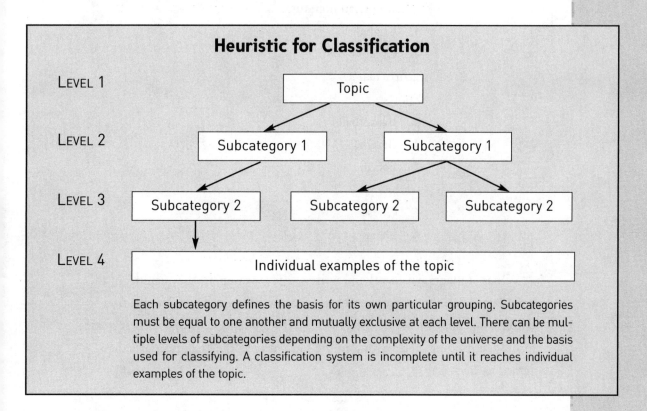

Heuristic for Classification

LEVEL 1 — Topic

LEVEL 2 — Subcategory 1 / Subcategory 1

LEVEL 3 — Subcategory 2 / Subcategory 2 / Subcategory 2

LEVEL 4 — Individual examples of the topic

Each subcategory defines the basis for its own particular grouping. Subcategories must be equal to one another and mutually exclusive at each level. There can be multiple levels of subcategories depending on the complexity of the universe and the basis used for classifying. A classification system is incomplete until it reaches individual examples of the topic.

Power Outline of School Activities

1. School Activities
    2. Curricular
        3. Math
            4. Algebra
            4. Calculus
        3. Science
            4. Chemistry
            4. Physical science
        3. Social studies
            4. Geography
            4. History
        3. Foreign languages
            4. German
            4. Chinese
        3. English
            4. American literature
            4. English I
            4. Creative writing
    2. Extracurricular
        3. Sports
            4. Basketball
            4. Baseball
            4. Soccer
        3. Clubs
            4. Chess
            4. Debate

Once students have read and written a few examples, they can begin to articulate criteria for a successful classification scheme. The Classification Criteria box shows a set of criteria that Jeff's students came up with; it guides reading, critiquing, and writing in the same way as the analytic scales discussed earlier.

Cursory Classification Introduction

Divide the following items of general topics into smaller, more specifically defined groups.

1. School

Divide into curricular and extracurricular on the power 2 level, and into humanities, sciences and maths, arts, and sports on the power 3 level.

English	biology	chemistry	basketball
drama	Spanish	health	algebra
newspaper	football	German	geometry
applied math	track	orchestra	physics
reading			

2. Library holdings

dictionaries	biography	nonfiction	short stories
autobiography	ballads	periodicals	reference
encyclopedias	history books	novels	poetry
travel	magazines	catalogues	thesauruses
fiction	historical fiction	odes	sonnets
newspapers			

3. Groceries

tomatoes	peaches	raspberries	chicken
basil	apples	pumpernickel rolls	strawberries
peppers	oregano	corned beef	rye bread
cranberries	pears	fish	chives
wheat buns	cookies	ice cream	milk
yogurt	butter cakes	bran muffins	allspice
cheese	green beans		

Getting It Right © 2007 by Michael W. Smith and Jeffrey D. Wilhelm, Scholastic Professional

Classification Criteria

A successful classification system will *identify*, *define*, *coordinate*, and *subordinate*.

IDENTIFY

1. Clearly identify the subject (the limited topic or universe) of the classification (top level of your issue tree).

DEFINE

2. Clearly define and explain the basis (the reasoning for dividing the universe into these particular classes). Ask yourself: Is the basis clearly worded?
3. Identify the purpose of the classification and the explanatory power and work such a classification can do for the audience.
   a. Who is the audience of the classification?
   b. How does the classification meet audience needs and interests?

COORDINATE

4. List the types (general classes) that will be explained and examined (this will be the second level of your issue tree). Ask yourself: Are all types at a given level of equal value? Are they mutually exclusive?

SUBORDINATE

5. Each subordinate layer of the classification fits under and is an example of the layer above it.
   a. Are all types at this level of equal value? Are they mutually exclusive?
   b. Do the types at each level of the issue tree comprehensively account for every member of the universe?
   c. Is each level more specific than the one above it?
6. The details (specific examples) are divided in terms of the basis.
7. Paragraphing and headers reflect the organization of the content and help the reader understand and navigate the text.
8. Transitions and key words are used to make the text coherent and navigable.
9. The examined types (the most specific examples at the bottom of the issue tree) are individual examples and are specifically shown to the reader.

CHANT IT, CURIOUS CLASSIFIERS: ALL GOOD CLASSIFICATIONS
IDENTIFY, DEFINE, COORDINATE, SUBORDINATE

Getting It Right

Once they have some expertise in the text structure, our students have great fun critiquing and writing ones that violate the rules. We have our students read the paragraph on the next page from Jorge Luis Borges (1952), which is a great model for an incorrect classification. In small groups, we ask them to critique the system, and then to write a fake classification based on the model (examples follow).

Student Analysis of Problems With Borges's Scheme
Celestial Emporium of Benevolent Knowledge

There is much to be desired in this system of classification. Its main problem is its inconsistencies and its overlapping; categories are not consistent.

A. Those that belong to the emperor
  1. Animals could be owned by the emperor and other people as well; not exclusive.
B. Embalmed ones
  2. The emperor could own a live animal while someone else owns a dead one; an animal could be embalmed in one case but alive in another.
  3. Technically, an embalmed animal is no longer an animal, since it is no longer alive.
C. Those that are trained
  4. The emperor could own a cat that was trained.
  5. Besides, what's the definition of "trained"?
D. Suckling pigs
  6. The emperor could own a trained suckling pig that is embalmed.
E. Mermaids
  7. No one has ever seen a mermaid and it probably doesn't exist, so why classify it as an animal?
  8. If they do exist, the emperor could own a trained suckling pig that was mistaken for a mermaid.
F. Fabulous ones
  9. Whose definition of *fabulous* are we using?
  10. The emperor might own a fabulous trained mermaid that embalms suckling pigs.

A Student's Incorrect Classification Following Borges Model

Homework can be (incorrectly) classified as:

A. Work that's too hard
B. Done on the bus home
C. Work that causes one to get bothersome rashes behind the ears and occasionally right above the hairline (English homework only)
D. Crumpled
E. Messily done
F. Late
G. Boring
H. Done while you have the walking flu
I. Done in pink ink
J. Stuff that no one can find a reason to learn or do except that it's required
K. Lost
L. Really, really stupid
M. Work done while somewhere in the world a cat is on the floor on a beach towel, and in Bizerte, Tunisia, the setting sun is at a 45° angle

[In] a certain Chinese encyclopedia entitled *Celestial Emporium of Benevolent Knowledge* . . . it is written that animals are divided into (a) those that belong to the Emperor, (b) embalmed ones, (c) those that are trained, (d) suckling pigs, (e) mermaids, (f) fabulous ones, (g) stray dogs, (h) those that are included in this classification, (i) those that tremble as if they were mad, (j) innumerable ones, (k) those drawn with a very fine camel's hair brush, (l) others, (m) those that have just broken a flower vase, (n) those that resemble flies from a distance.

Students also had fun analyzing, explaining, and transforming their silly, incorrect versions into classification schemes that fit the criteria. If students can successfully do this kind of work, they demonstrate their understanding of correct classification schemes.

Using a modeling sequence such as this can help writers develop a sense of global text structure that will lend purpose and coherence to their writing at the sentence, paragraph, and text levels.

As we were composing this section on classification, we worried a bit that we might be straying too far afield from our emphasis on correctness. So we thought it would be a good idea to offer an explanation of why we decided to keep it. In the first place, recall that students' lack of confidence is one common cause of problems with correctness. The kind of work on text structure we're proposing should make students much more confident when they compose their classifications. Second, the analysis of features allowed us to embed instruction in correctness into a meaningful context. For example, as we discussed conceptual parallelism in numbers 4 and 5 of the preceding classification criteria, we could also talk about grammatical parallelism. As we talked about signaling the relationship among levels of the power outline, we could talk about and give students practice in producing the grammatical structures that writers use to signal coordination versus subordination. As we have suggested throughout this book, it's important to make instruction part of meaningful work on writing.

When responding to and evaluating students, always keep these principles in mind:

Principles for Promoting Confidence and Self-Efficacy

▶ Communicate always that the writer has the ultimate authority and decision-making power over her work (e.g., with the word-processing peer revision sheets).

▶ Provide time and support for peer editing and revision.

▶ Use PQP for peer and teacher response to student writing: **P**raise first, then **Q**uestion, then offer suggestions for **P**olishing.

▶ Begin a response to student writing by citing what you like; couch suggestions as "I wonder what would happen if . . ."

▶ Don't mark all errors, only the few that you are focusing on with the class (or with that student).

▶ Mark errors in the margin and have students do the correcting.

▶ Always allow for improvements and revisions at any time.

Overreliance on Technology

Another source of errors is students' overreliance on technology. Now that university students write papers using word processors, we don't get as many spelling errors as we used to, but we get many more homonym errors. We think the reason is that students count on their computers to do their proofreading for them.

Addressing such errors requires a thoughtful analysis of the limitations of electronic tools. Spell-checks flag names and unfamiliar words (e.g., *spell-check*) but can't catch homonym confusion. A class and personal spelling list that includes often misused homonyms is a great way of encouraging students to double-check their spell-checks.

Grammar checks catch fragments, but they can't determine whether fragments are intentional. One great way to evaluate the power and limitations of a grammar check is to use it on a wide range of texts, from those produced by the class to such famous texts as the Gettysburg Address, and to discuss the merit (or demerit!) of the suggestions it makes.

Not Knowing the Rule

Sometimes the source of an error is not knowing the rule. In those cases students have to be taught the rule, but they have to be taught deeply and with an inquiry orientation so that they construct their own understandings of the reasons and story behind the rule. And, of course, they have to be given lots of practice applying the rule. For example, when Michael taught ninth grade, all of his students were native speakers of English. They made very few subject-verb agreement errors. Virtually all of them occurred when they used a plural verb with a singular subject that was followed by a prepositional phrase with a plural object (e.g., "Every one of the boys have had a chance to play.").

Michael addressed this error by having students with this problem cross out all of the words that separated subjects from their predicates and then check that their verb choice was correct. (If students use a highlighter to do their crossing out, this doesn't interfere with subsequent revision.) Because Michael's students did not speak a dialect with different agreement rules, this was typically enough to solve the problem. Dawn Duperre, one of Michael's former students, developed a motto for teaching this rule to her students: "When in doubt, cross it out." To make sure students had learned the rule, subject-verb agreement was one of the major foci of Michael's attention to correctness for several papers.

Jeff and his student teachers created a more elaborate sequence. When Jeff's students studied the problem of agreement (both subject-verb and pronoun-antecedent), they found a similar source of difficulty. Once again, the most common problem occurred in sentences in which there was a clause or phrase between the subject and the verb. The students were matching the verb to the closest noun rather than to the subject of the sentence. If the closest noun differed from the subject in its singularity or plurality, then subject-verb disagreement was the result.

The second most common problem was using words such as *each*, *everyone*, *everybody*, *someone*, and *somebody* as plural nouns. (And sometimes both problems occur in one sentence, as in "Each of the boys have to go to detention.") Taken together, these two problems accounted for more than 80 percent of the subject-verb agreement problems in students' writing.

As a consequence, it made sense to tackle these two issues with students rather than have them devote time to work sheets that addressed other causes. To focus on other causes and manifestations, we think, would be a misuse of energy, unless done individually with particular students whose agreement errors have different causes.

Jeff's students worked to get their middle schoolers to determine agreement rules by giving them incorrect and correct examples. Following are some examples and the kind of rule we hope the students will articulate after comparing correct and incorrect examples.

Incorrect:
Everyone absolutely must do their own safety check before getting
    on the raft.

The failure to complete a thorough safety check while listening to
    your iPod and singing out loud and dancing are not in any way
    surprising.

Someone left their life preserver on the shore after loading their raft
    with gear.

Correct:

Everyone absolutely must do his or her own safety check before getting on the raft.

The failure to complete a thorough safety check while listening to your iPod and singing out loud and dancing is not in any way surprising.

Someone left his or her life preserver on the shore after loading the raft with gear.

Rule One: *Each, either, every, everybody, everyone, somebody,* and *someone* are singular and stand for one person or thing. In writing, they must take a singular verb and a singular pronoun. Circle your choices.

Every player on the team has their/his hair shaved off.

Each starter must play with their/her shin guards and mouth guard.

Someone from one of the teams have/has to use his/their stopwatch.

Rule Two: When there is a group of words between *each, either, every, everybody, everyone, somebody, someone,* and *one* and its pronoun, be really sure to keep the verb and pronoun consistent with the subject! Circle your choices.

Each of the final projects are/is really difficult.

Each of my horses have/has its/their own stall.

One of the cars from the stock car races were/was really wrecked.

One of the girls aren't/isn't wearing their/her own shoes.

Lots of rock groups like the Fray has/have a really great bass guitarist.

Rule Three: When a group of words separates the subject and predicate, cross them out to see if the subject and predicate agree. Make sure that the subject and predicate are both singular or both plural.

The following boxes (Inductive Exercises for Understanding Apostrophe Use and Inductive Exercises for Understanding Semicolon Use) give two more examples of how we tried to promote the kind of deep learning of rules that we are calling for. Jeff's student teacher Steven Wells used both while he and his students were reading *Into the Wild* by Jon Krakauer in a unit that considered the question, "What are the costs of conformity and nonconformity?"

Inductive Exercises for Understanding Apostrophe Use

Apostrophe Use

What do you notice about the use of the possessive apostrophe in the following sentences from the book? See any patterns? Clue: Check out these italicized words!

> Given *Walt's* **need** to exert control and *Chris's* extravagantly independent **nature**, polarization was inevitable. (p. 64)

> Franz occupied *McCandless's* old **campsite**, just past the hot springs. (p. 58)

> How I feed myself is none of the *government's* **business**. (p. 6)

What do you notice about the pattern of italicized words?

How are the italicized words related to the words in bold?

What should we remember?

What is the proofreading tool these sentences provide us?

Now, let's apply what you've learned. Write three sentences in which you show possession, and not the demonic kind!

> Examples: Gallien thought the *hitchhiker's* **scheme** was foolhardy. (p. 5)
> Mr. Wilhelm thinks that skiing up Schaefer Butte is an endurance *athlete's* **dream**.

1.

2.

3.

Hey, Super Student! _____

Your name here!

_____

Language tool you are learning to wield

Continues

Getting It Right © 2007 by Michael W. Smith and Jeffrey D. Wilhelm, Scholastic Professional

In a previous exercise, you learned where and how to use a possessive apostrophe: first noun + ' + s followed by a second noun. Only nouns can possess nouns. No verbs allowed! And when it comes to the possessing noun and the possessed noun, you can't have one without the other. Now read these sentences. What do you notice about the use of the plural possessive apostrophe? Hint: Check out what is italicized!

> The *families'* **hot tubs** all accommodated at least six people.
> The room was filled with the *puppies'* **whining**.
> Not all of *children's* fantasy **books** are violent.
> The *women's* former **neighbor** stopped by to visit.

What do you notice about the use of the plural possessive apostrophe?

What should you remember?

What is the proofreading key?

Try some yourself as you write me a brief note about who is responsible for our school's tremendous school spirit!

Contractions and Apostrophes

1. Yes, contractions are what your mother had before you made your entrance!
2. No, these are not the kind of contractions we are discussing here!

We are talking about contracting language, that is, making it shorter and quicker. Contractions are words in which letters have been omitted and replaced with the apostrophe; this not to be confused with the apostrophe for possession!

Notice the following transformations:

Do not = don't

I am = I'm

He will = he'll

Who is = who's

Should not = shouldn't

Could have = could've

What changes occur to create a contraction?

When and where do you use contractions?

Given what you have noticed, contract the following:

1. She will

2. It is

3. They have

4. They are

Consider this example from *Into the Wild*:

I fear that *you'll* ignore my advice. You think I'm stubborn, but *you're* even more stubborn than me. (p. 57)

Uncontracted: I fear that you will ignore my advice. You think I am stubborn, but you are even more stubborn than me.

What is the effect of each? Which version do you think is best and most powerful to use at this point in the book?

Getting It Right © 2007 by Michael W. Smith and Jeffrey D. Wilhelm, Scholastic Professional

Inductive Exercises for Understanding Semicolon Use

What do you notice about the use of the semicolon and the positioning of *however* in the following sentences?

> Most singers gain fame through hard work and dedication; however, Evita found other means.

> Most singers gain fame though hard work and dedication; Evita, however, found other means.

> She doubted the value of daily medication; however, she decided to try it.

> She doubted the value of daily medication; she decided, however, to try it.

Can you identify how the positioning of *however* relates to the use of the semicolon? Study the parts of the sentence carefully. Can you determine the significance of the semicolon?

Now apply what you have learned to sentences that you wrote in your own essays:

> Every genius has his or her own style, however, some generalities have appeared between some types of geniuses.

> Similarly, every creature had control over his/her own body, however, each creature, showed some form of symbiosis with its natural environment.

> He seems to always be one or two decades behind in the fashion curve, however, it's OK to include a random article from an expensive source per outfit.

Explain your reasons for using the semicolon and/or changing the position of *however*.

How has changing the placement of the semicolon changed the meaning?

Getting It Right © 2007 by Michael W. Smith and Jeffrey D. Wilhelm, Scholastic Professional

Another way to help students understand a rule, the need for it, and its effect on meaning is to provide examples that show students how mechanics and conventions change the meaning of the same set of words. In J. N. Hook and W. H. Evans's *The Teaching of High School English* (1982) and Maxwell Nurnberg's *Questions You Always Wanted to Ask About English (but Were Afraid to Raise Your Hand)* (1972), the authors offer examples such as the following:

> Legend has it that the Czarina of Russia saw a note on the desk of Alexander III that read:
> "Pardon impossible; to be sent to Siberia." She changed the punctuation to: "Pardon; impossible to be sent to Siberia!"

You can also demonstrate the importance of punctuation by providing sentences that make no sense without it.

Ask students to punctuate the following so that they make sense:

> That that is is that that is not is not is not that it it is
> (That that is, is; that that is not, is not. Is not that it? It is!)

> While I was dressing my little brother came in
> (While I was dressing, my little brother came in.)

> Lord Wellington entered on his head a helmet on his feet a pair of well-polished boots on his brow a cloud in his hand his favorite walking stick in his eye fire
> (Lord Wellington entered; on his head a helmet, on his feet a pair of well-polished boots, on his brow a cloud, in his hand his favorite walking stick, in his eye fire.)

How are the meanings of the two sentences in the pairs below different, and how are the different meanings conveyed through the punctuation?

> Woman! Without her, man would be a savage.
> Woman without her man would be a savage.

> Beth, thinks her employer, is attractive.
> Beth thinks her employer is attractive.

Mr. Smith, the superintendent came in.
Mr. Smith, the superintendent, came in.

"Brad," called Miles, "Come here!"
Brad called, "Miles, come here!"

The tight-rope walker almost fell.
The tight rope-walker almost fell.

No man can be happy.
No. Man can be happy.

Hypercorrectness

Another common cause of error is hypercorrectness, an overemphasis on being correct. It typically occurs in two forms. One is the overapplication of a newly learned rule, structure, or punctuation mark. A classic example that many teachers have experienced is the overuse of *'s*. Even after a lesson as extensive as the one we just shared, some students are sure to use apostrophes for every single word that ends in *s*. Another example is found among students who have never used articles before, either in their home language or in English. When they first begin to use them, they'll almost always overuse them. For some students, overusing a new convention seems to be part of the process of learning it.

So what to do? The first thing is to recognize hypercorrectness for what it is: students working hard to do what they think the teacher wants. Circling every extra apostrophe or article is certainly not appropriate under those circumstances. Initially, a reminder might help: "Remember, use apostrophes only when you want to show possession. Plurals don't take apostrophes." A reference to the spelling rules sheet from Chapter 3 might help.

> "Recognize hypercorrectness for what it is: students working hard to do what they think the teacher wants."

Sometimes students will correct themselves. If not, asking them to produce the structure in sentence combining exercises and to attend to the overapplication of the rule in their editing will likely help. As we said earlier, if students are new to Standard English, it probably makes sense to wait and see what happens as their command of SE increases. Also, it is always essential to have students inquire into how and why language works as it does (e.g., what an apostrophe can designate and mean; how a semicolon creates a relationship between what precedes and follows it), and to help students inquire into their own language use.

A second kind of hypercorrectness error results from attempting to sound more educated. The classic example of such an error is "between you and I," which seems to sound fancier to many students than does the correct "between you and me." Another example is a construction like this one: "I didn't know whom was going to be there." Students who overuse *whom* are likely doing so because they're trying to sound smart.

We think this kind of hypercorrectness may have its root in students not trusting their own instincts. And if they don't, we may be at fault. Think of all the things that students have been told about formal academic writing: "Don't use *I*." "Don't start a sentence with a conjunction." "Try not to use forms of *to be*." (We have continually violated all of these mythrules throughout this book.) Teaching students these mythrules also teaches them that their experience with and intuitions about language aren't to be trusted.

Remember that episode on *Seinfeld* in which George decides that the way for him to succeed with women, on the job, in every endeavor, in fact, is to decide what to do and then do the opposite? We worry that the emphasis on rules, many of which are not grounded in the way writers actually behave, develops an analogous consciousness in students.

Mistakes that are rooted in this kind of hypercorrectness would typically be low on the list in anyone's hierarchy of errors. But if you plan to address them, once again, you'll need to address the cause: the students' feeling that what sounds right must be wrong. Having your students analyze mythrules might be one way of doing so. Having them revise texts that are overly formal into effective plainspeak is another.

A Model Sequence: Learning to Proofread

Each year, Jeff spends just a bit of time near the end of his first writing assignment sequence to teach his students general strategies in how to proofread. He then proceeds to highlight proofreading for one or two particular kinds of errors.

First, he provides students with one of those picture searches in which you look for items that are hidden within a larger drawing, perhaps little spies in the drapery and carpeting of a picture of an embassy.

The kids always experience some initial difficulty. Jeff lets them struggle for a few moments and then he puts the puzzle on the overhead and circles one or two of the spies. He then asks the students what the spies look like (they all had gangster caps, masks around their eyes, and fat faces) and where they are likely to hide (in areas with lots of lines and circular designs, like the drapes, picture frame, and carpeting). After this brainstorm, the students quickly were able to find the other spies.

Jeff points out to the students that this is exactly what they must do when they proofread. They need to (1) know what the errors they tend to make look like and (2) where to look for them. (Throughout this book, we've tried to alert you to both of these things.)

Jeff then tells the students that in the paper they are currently writing, all students will proofread their own and each other's papers for one or two particular errors, like fragments, as an example. To do so, they need to know what they look like (they start with a beware word) and where they tend to lurk (in a sentence with a promise word). With these two kinds of knowledge about a particular error, students can successfully proofread for them.

To equip her students with the requisite proofreading knowledge for particular kinds of sentence constructions, Jeff's student teacher Denise Braswell, whom we met last chapter, came up with the clever idea of casting students as CSIs (Correct Sentence Investigators) in dramatic scenarios that would engage and encourage them to proofread for these errors.

Denise told her students that you can't find errors in a paper unless you know where to look and what to look for—that is, unless you know proofreading cues. Although she made it clear that content was her first concern for their writing, she told them that language correctness was important because it serves to make and communicate meaning as well as portray the writer's identity.

She stressed that revision consists of moving, adding, and changing big ideas and pieces of text—it goes deep. Proofreading is part of the editing process—the final polish or surface touches on a piece to make it sing and gleam.

Denise had students write from an appropriate model. Here's one that's good not only for helping students with using the comma (and the dash) in cumulative descriptions, but also with careful observation, characterization, and painting images with participles (see Noden, 1999).

Old Florist

By Theodore Roethke

<u>That</u> hump <u>of a man [woman, athlete, etc.]</u> bunching chrysanthemums,
<u>or</u> pinching back asters<u>,</u> <u>or</u> planting azaleas,
tamp<u>ing and</u> stamp<u>ing</u> dirt into pots—
<u>how he [she] could</u> flick and pick

rotten leaves <u>or</u> yellowy petals,
<u>or</u> scoop out a weed close to the flourishing roots,
<u>or</u> make the dust buzz with a light spray,
<u>or</u> drown a bug in one spit of tobacco juice,
<u>or</u> fan life into wilted sweet peas with his hat,
<u>or</u> stand all night watering roses, <u>his [her]</u> feet blue in rubber boots.

After reading the poem, students used the underlined words as a frame for their own portrayal of a particular person from the setting they were describing. This description could then be inserted into their sensoriums (see Chapter 2). A variation of this technique is to have students choose a description from their writing and boil it down or transform it into a poem using a model like the preceding one. (See Scholes, 1981.)

Denise, a sophisticated teacher who believed her students were up for it, also wanted to demonstrate to them that sometimes a writer might use run-on or fragment sentences for effect, and that it was okay for them to do so only if they had a particular reason they could justify. (She also reminded her students that they shouldn't try it on the state writing test!)

She chose to have students write following the model of Sandra Cisneros's description of hair from *The House on Mango Street* (1984, pp. 6–7).

Everybody in our family has different hair. My Papa's hair is like a broom, all up in the air. And me, my hair is lazy. It never obeys barrettes or bands. Carlos' hair is thick and straight. He doesn't need to comb it. Nenny's hair is slippery—slides right out of your hand. And Kiki, who is the youngest, has hair like fur.

But my mother's hair, my mother's hair, like little rosettes, like little candy circles all curly and pretty because she pinned it in pincurls all day, sweet to put your nose into when she is holding you, holding you and you feel safe, is the warm smell of bread before you bake it, is the smell when she makes room for you on her side of the bed still warm from her skin, and you sleep near her, the rain outside falling and Papa snoring. The snoring, the rain, and Mama's hair that smells like bread.

Denise asked her students to make lists of everything they notice about each of the two paragraphs, and how they differ. Think of all the things that can be taught from this short exercise: the effect of sentence length and variety, the powerful use of fragments for effect, voice, comparison and contrast, use of specific examples, sensory description (all relevant to Denise's current unit), and much more.

Again, the teacher can provide an example of how to write from the model, then brainstorm with students for other items they can describe: houses, shoes, trees, and so on.

Finally, Denise had the whole class work on inductive exercises for one language tool so that students could figure out how it worked and then apply it to proofreading their own papers. For her descriptive writing unit, she focused on the use of introductory elements in a sentence. But you could choose anything at all for your focus. The inductive exercises for semicolon and apostrophe or subject-verb agreement and quotations in this chapter provide examples.

Denise also had students set up stations for one error they had chosen to personally become an expert on. Other students could come visit them and get their paper proofread for that particular error. Cast as CSI agents, the students completed a CSI Log for a model error. Then they completed one for each error of that kind they found in the papers they proofread. The logs included the crime, the evidence of the crime, the causes of it, and the corrective or justice. They also state the law (the rule) for that kind of sentence.

Here's an example of a log filed by three Correct Sentence Investigators. You'll find a blank form on the next page.

CSI Log

Agents: Chance, Sienna, and Aurora

Crime: Failure to punctuate dialogue correctly

Evidence: Mr. Lynn said "That will help."

Law-Abiding Citizen (correct model): Mr. Lynn said, "That will help."

Causes: Not understanding that what is being said needs to be separated from who is saying it

Tip-offs/Clues: Dialogue is present with no commas.

Justice (correcting the crime): Put a comma before or after dialogue, depending on where the dialogue is placed in the sentence.

What the Law States: Use commas (and quotes) to set off the exact words of the speaker from the rest of the sentence.

Exceptions: Do not use a comma or quotation marks for indirect quotes.

Example: Mr. Lynn says that doing this will help.

Denise had great fun with her unit, and so did her students. She used crime scene tape around the classroom, wore a lab coat, and added the title "Agent" to students' names. After the short proofreading unit, some of the students wanted to continue to be called "Agent." Some wanted promotions for their good work: One boy wanted to be called "Special Agent"! It just goes to show that even proofreading and editing can be taught in interesting and engaging ways that lead to true understanding!

Correct Sentence Investigators (CSI) Log

Agents:

Crime:

Evidence:

Law-Abiding Citizen (correct model):

Causes:

Tip-offs/Clues:

Justice (correcting the crime):

What the Law States:

Exceptions:

Example:

Getting It Right © 2007 by Michael W. Smith and Jeffrey D. Wilhelm, Scholastic Professional

Conclusion

We haven't offered an exhaustive list of all of the possible sources of error, though we hope the ones we have identified here are useful to you. Rather, we hope we have convinced you that the only errors that can be effectively addressed with a red pencil are careless errors (what are called performance-based errors). In our experience, the vast majority of students' errors didn't stem from carelessness but rather from some other cause (in other words, they were knowledge-based errors of some kind). Once we had determined those causes, it was relatively easy to design instruction to address them. (And even with carelessness, giving attention to the error—by putting it on a proofreading list or teaching kids how to proofread—makes the kids less careless.) When we devised instruction, we made sure to focus students' attention on the particular error we were working on and to give them enough practice so that they could become comfortable with the tools we provided them. And, we're happy to say, our students, slowly but surely, began to write more correctly.

Instructional Principles

▸ Identify the potential cause of the error.

▸ Address one error/issue at a time.

▸ Use examples from your students' own writing to show them that their learning will pay off in the here and now.

▸ If students' home language is not Standard English, use their home languages and dialects for comparisons and contrastive examples, explicitly using what they already know to approach the new challenge.

▸ Show how the error makes a difference to meaning and can affect the reader's perception of the writer.

▸ Develop and apply a heuristic, or proofreading and problem-solving strategy, that applies to the issue.

▸ Provide plenty of practice within a context of use.

▸ Immediately apply the strategy in real writing that matters to kids.

Chapter 5

Will It Work in the Real World?

One of Michael's best friends was complaining to him the other day about her son Adam's English teacher. "They've only read one book all year," she said, "and they haven't written any papers at all." What had they been doing? Much of their time was spent on grammar. And that's a shame, for a wealth of research has established beyond question that traditional school grammar, characterized by defining and labeling the parts of a sentence, does not help students write better or more correctly.

So why does the teaching of Traditional School Grammar still have such a large place in so many schools? We think it's because English teachers recognize the importance of writing correctly (even if we are more sensitive to error than the general public is). High-stakes writing assessments put external pressure on teachers to help their students become better writers and editors. Many teachers, we believe, think it's common sense that teaching grammar will help them achieve these goals. But sometimes the common sense doesn't make any sense. Such is the case with the teaching of grammar.

That's why through the course of this book we've made the following recommendations:

> ➤ Teach only the terms that kids really need to know and teach them well.

- Teach those terms when students need them in a way that proves why they are important.
- Develop a hierarchy of errors and address the errors at the top of the hierarchy one by one, making sure that you provide enough time for students to master what you've taught them.
- Share the responsibility for teaching across grade levels. Don't reteach the same things every year (and don't move too quickly because you are trying to do too much—do less to do more and to do it more thoroughly).
- Identify the causes of the errors you plan to address and design instruction that addresses those causes.

Let's test to see whether our recommendations make sense in today's policy environment. The new SAT would seem to be a good vehicle for such a test, since it's taken by students across the country. The question would then be, How would the recommendations we have made serve a school or district that has set improving SAT scores as a goal?

The short answer: quite well. In the first place, the new SAT requires students to do some actual writing. Students may get only 25 minutes, but they do have to write. According to the College Board (n.d.), an essay that gets a 6 has the following qualities:

- It effectively and insightfully develops a point of view on the issue and demonstrates outstanding critical thinking, using clearly appropriate examples, reasons, and other evidence to support its position.
- It is well organized and clearly focused, demonstrating clear coherence and smooth progression of ideas.
- It exhibits skillful use of language, using a varied, accurate, and apt vocabulary.
- It demonstrates meaningful variety in sentence structure.
- It is free of most errors in grammar, usage, and mechanics.

These criteria are heavily weighted toward the production of discourse. That is, composing seems to be more important than correcting. There is only one bullet on correctness, and this criterion makes it clear that the essay can exhibit some errors. The Princeton Review's stated goal is to help students "crack" the SAT (Robinson & Katzman, 2005). Their advice on cracking the writing section is "don't sweat the small stuff, but do sweat the structure and develop your thesis" (p. 310). It seems clear, then, that we can prepare kids to do well on the writing section of the SAT by helping them write organized and well-developed essays. (You can see Smith & Wilhelm, 2006, chap. 5, for more of our ideas on instructional strategies to do just that.)

Not even the staunchest proponent of traditional school grammar could argue that the SAT is designed to test students' knowledge of grammatical terms, so advocates of TSG would have to argue that being able to provide definitions, to diagram sentences, or to label sentences and/or their parts would help students compose. For example, they might argue that labeling sentence types helps students do well on the fourth criterion. However, the evidence doesn't bear them out. Research does not demonstrate that studying traditional school grammar helps kids write more maturely. On the other hand, the research is unequivocal that sentence combining does indeed increase students' syntactic maturity.

But one bullet point does talk about correctness, and there is a whole section of the Princeton Review's manual called "Grammar." How about that section? First, it is important to note that *none* of the multiple-choice writing questions on the ETS Web site and *none* of the myriad sample questions provided by the Princeton Review in *Cracking the New SAT* (Robinson & Katzman, 2005) employ *any* technical vocabulary. That means that test takers don't have to define a part of speech or underline the subject or predicate of a sentence. They don't have to diagram a sentence.

They do have to recognize errors and be able to make rhetorical choices that improve the quality of writing that others have done, especially by eliminating wordiness or redundancy and increasing clarity. So maybe extensive study of grammatical terms would help here.

Nope. *Cracking the New SAT* puts it this way:

> To do well on the Writing section, you need to remember some basic grammar rules. Now don't get worked up about being tested on grammar. SAT grammar is not difficult, nor is it extensive. In fact the Writing section really only tests five basic grammatical concepts:

1. verbs, 2. nouns, 3. pronouns, 4. prepositions, 5. other little things. (p. 278)

If you think back to Chapter 2, you'll see that *Cracking the New SAT*'s list of terms is even shorter than ours. To be fair, the authors do talk about other concepts when they spin out their discussion of their list of five. When the authors talk about nouns, they add the terms *singular*, *plural*, and *collective*. When they talk about verbs, they talk about tense, agreement, and parallelism. When they talk about pronouns, they talk again about agreement, add the idea of case, and stress the importance of reducing ambiguity. The other little things include faulty comparisons, misplaced modifiers, and a number of commonly confused word pairs (e.g., *elicit* and *illicit*). But that's it.

If a school distributed responsibility for teaching these issues across grades, teachers would have plenty of time to teach all of them deeply. In Chapter 3 we propose one possible sequence. But as we said, we think it's far more important that teachers share the burden than that they share it in any particular way.

Even with such sharing, teachers might have to do some reviewing, at least with individuals. They might have to introduce new conventions as students produce more complex structures. They might have to teach more than just their primary foci if the writing their students were doing required understandings they hadn't yet developed. But by narrowing the primary responsibilities of each grade, teachers could teach deeply whatever correctness issues they address and still have time for plenty of reading and writing. We think that Adam and his mother would be delighted with such a plan.

We realize that for many of our readers, however, the test they feel most responsible for is the state test. Tests vary from state to state, so we encourage all teachers to look hard at their state standards and state test to determine just what they ask. Let's take our two states as examples.

Pennsylvania requires students to both compose a paper and respond to multiple-choice editing questions. Let's look at the paper first. The state's scoring guidelines say that 80 percent of the score depends on its content and organization and only 20 percent on conventions. The sample multiple-choice questions on the state's Web site ask students to make judgments about a number of word choice, organizational, and punctuation issues. Only one question contains a technical term. It asks students to indicate which word in a sentence is an adjective.

It's quite clear that the state of Pennsylvania does not endorse the kind of grammar instruction that prevails in schools. In fact, its professional development materials cite George Hillocks as saying that none of the studies he reviewed "provides any support for teaching grammar as a means of improving composition skill" (1986, p. 138).

Idaho's writing assessment for seventh graders is scored holistically on the basis of six areas of consideration: ideas, organization, voice, word choice, sentence fluency, and correctness. The descriptor for proficient achievement in correctness reads, "Errors in grammar, spelling and conventions do not interfere with understanding." A number of things are noteworthy here. First, the descriptor presumes that papers will contain some errors. Second, as we argued in Chapter 3, very few errors interfere with meaning. If Idaho middle school teachers were looking for a reason to focus on only a few significant errors, the state seems to provide it.

Idaho's Department of Education does not have sample items for its language test available, as it is currently being revised. Previous tests, however, have included more technical vocabulary than the test in Pennsylvania does. Idaho's Department of Education does provide teachers with a list of concepts that students are expected to master. The seventh-grade language arts concepts differ from the ones we propose in Chapter 2 only because they include four kinds of nouns (proper, common, concrete, and abstract), three kinds of verbs (action, linking, and helping), and different sentence types. There's nothing about verbals. Or the different kinds and cases of pronouns. Or any of the myriad other technical terms that exist in the study of TSG. Moreover, none of the writing standards call for students to be able to label or analyze a piece of writing. Instead they call for students to produce their own writing effectively.

To be sure, a teacher in Idaho might feel the need to spend more time on technical vocabulary than a teacher in Pennsylvania should. (This may change with the revised test, as one of the major suggestions teachers in Idaho made was to reduce the amount of technical vocabulary.) But we're afraid that teachers in both states are spending a disproportionate amount of time on grammar work sheets when it's clear that the students' own writing is substantially more important. Embedding focused instruction in grammar in contexts in which kids get repeated practice writing meaningful texts would seem to better serve everyone involved.

We know that our recommendations will make some of our readers nervous. Both of us have been in situations where teachers have raised concerns about our "less is more" approach. Some have insisted that knowledge of traditional school grammar is a prerequisite for effective writing and speaking. Some have said, "If I don't mark every error, aren't I teaching them to write incorrectly—or at least implicitly endorsing it?" Some have wondered how they'll be able to communicate with their students without an extensive common grammatical vocabulary.

In every school in which we've heard those concerns, we've also heard complaints that kids just aren't writing well. It's time to face the facts: The old ways just aren't working. They haven't worked in the past. They aren't working now. They won't work in the future. It's time to make some changes. We hope this book helps in that effort.

APPENDIX A
Oakland Board of Education Amended Resolution on AAVE/Ebonics

WHEREAS, numerous validated scholarly studies demonstrate that African-American students as a part of their culture and history as African people possess and utilize a language described in various scholarly approaches as "Ebonics" (literally "Black sounds") or "Pan African Communication Behaviors" or "African Language Systems"; and

WHEREAS, these studies have also demonstrated that African Language Systems have origins in West and Niger-Congo languages and are not merely dialects of English; and

WHEREAS, these studies demonstrate that such West and Niger-Congo African languages have been recognized and addressed in the educational community as worthy of study, understanding and application of their principles, laws and structures for the benefit of African-American students both in terms of positive appreciation of the language and these students' acquisition and mastery of English language skills; and

WHEREAS, such recognition by scholars has given rise over the past fifteen years to legislation passed by the State of California recognizing the unique language stature of descendants of slaves, with such legislation being prejudicially and unconstitutionally vetoed repeatedly by various California state governors; and

WHEREAS, judicial cases in states other than California have recognized the unique language stature of African-American pupils, and such recognition by courts has resulted in court-mandated educational programs which have substantially benefited African-American children in the interest of vindicating their equal protection of the law rights under the Fourteenth Amendment to the United States Constitution; and

WHEREAS, the Federal Bilingual Education Act (20 U.S.C. 1402 et seq.) mandates that local educational agencies "build their capacities to establish, implement and sustain programs of instruction for children and youth of limited English proficiency"; and

WHEREAS, the interest of the Oakland Unified School District in providing equal opportunities for all of its students dictate limited English proficient educational programs recognizing the English language acquisition and improvement skills of African-American students are as fundamental as is application of bilingual or second language learner principles for others whose primary languages are other than English. Primary languages are the language patterns children bring to school; and

WHEREAS, the standardized tests and grade scores of African-American students in reading and language arts skills measuring their application of English skills are substantially below state and national norms and that such deficiencies will be remedied by application of a program featuring African Language Systems principles to move students from the language patterns they bring to school to English proficiency; and

WHEREAS, standardized tests and grade scores will be remedied by application of a program that teachers and instructional assistants, who are certified in the methodology of African Language Systems principles used to transition students from the language patterns they bring to school to English. The certified teachers of these students will be provided incentives including, but not limited to salary differentials;

NOW, THEREFORE, BE IT RESOLVED that the Board of Education officially recognizes the existence, and the cultural and historic bases of West and Niger-Congo African Language Systems, and each language as the primary language of many African-American students; and

BE IT FURTHER RESOLVED that the Board of Education hereby adopts the report, recommendations and attached Policy Statement of the District's African-American Task Force on the language stature of African-American speech; and

BE IT FURTHER RESOLVED that the Superintendent in conjunction with her staff shall immediately devise and implement the best possible academic program for the combined purposes of facilitating the acquisition and mastery of English language skills, while respecting and embracing the legitimacy and richness of the language patterns whether they are known as "Ebonics", "African Language Systems", "Pan African Communication Behaviors", or other description; and

BE IT FURTHER RESOLVED that the Board of Education hereby commits to earmark District general and special funding as is reasonably necessary and appropriate to enable the Superintendent and her staff to accomplish the fore-going; and

BE IT FURTHER RESOLVED that the Superintendent and her staff shall utilize the input of the entire Oakland educational community as well as state and federal scholarly and educational input in devising such a program; and

BE IT FURTHER RESOLVED that periodic reports on the progress of the creation and implementation of such an educational program shall be made to the Board of Education at least once per month commencing at the Board meeting of December 18, 1996.

APPENDIX B
Homonyms and Other Frequently Confused/Misused Words

1. **a – an**

    Use *an* before vowel sounds except long *u*: <u>an</u> uncle

    Use *a* before consonant sounds and long *u*: <u>a</u> uniform

2. **accept – except**

    accept = to take or willingly receive

    except = with the exclusion of

    > I <u>accept</u> your present of a fruit basket. I enjoyed everything <u>except</u> the prunes, which do not agree with me.

3. **advice – advise**

    > I <u>advise</u> you to take Mr. Wilhelm's mature <u>advice</u>.

4. **affect – effect**

    affect (verb) = to change or influence

    > Did his illness <u>affect</u> his running ability?

    effect (noun) = the result

    > The <u>effect</u> of Swen's accident was not serious, Bill.

    effect (verb) = to bring about or produce

    > It will be difficult to <u>effect</u> a complete transformation and turn them all into sophisticated students.

5. **aggravate – annoy**

    aggravate = to make worse

    > Jumping up and down will <u>aggravate</u> your knee injury.

    annoy = to bother

    > Your squeaky metallic voice <u>annoys</u> me.

6. **allusion – illusion**

   allusion = reference

   > Brad made an <u>allusion</u> to Cervantes's *Don Quixote*.

   illusion = false idea

   > The man shattered Raina's <u>illusions</u> about warfare and romance.

7. **a lot – alot**

   Two words: a lot

8. **aloud – allowed**

   aloud = audibly; allowed = permitted

   > You are not <u>allowed</u> to speak <u>aloud</u> in the library.

9. **altar – alter**

   altar = raised structure used in worship or ritual

   > The acolytes lighted the candles on the <u>altar</u>.

   alter = to change

   > The tall ship must <u>alter</u> its course to enter the harbor.

10. **amount – number**

    Use *number* for things that can be counted and *amount* for things that are measured but cannot be counted.

    > There are <u>fewer</u> apples in my basket, and they will make <u>less</u> cider.

11. **anecdote – antidote**

    anecdote = story

    > Ms. Viegel enjoys telling humorous <u>anecdotes</u>.

    antidote = remedy to counteract poison

    > Is there an <u>antidote</u> to the poisonous bite of the black widow?

12. **any body – anybody**

    > Did <u>anybody</u> (any persons at all) see <u>any body</u> lying in the ditch around Halloween?

13. are – or – our

are = linking verb

> We <u>are</u> West Junior High students.

or = conjunction

> Brad <u>or</u> Miles will win the spitting contest.

our = possessive pronoun

> <u>Our</u> teacher is suave.

14. bath – bathe, lath – lathe, teeth – teethe, cloth – clothe, loath – loathe, lithe, writhe, tithe

> To take a <u>bath</u> is to <u>bathe</u>. Pieces of <u>lath</u> are never put into a <u>lathe</u>. A child about to <u>teethe</u> will soon have <u>teeth</u>. <u>Clothe</u> yourself in garb of <u>cloth</u>. I am <u>loath</u> to tell you how much I <u>loathe</u> Elton John's music. The <u>lithe</u> wrestler caused his opponent to <u>writhe</u> in agony. A <u>tithe</u> (one tenth) of his income goes to philanthropy.

15. beauty – beautiful

> Use *beautiful* as an adjective. *Beauty* is the noun (not *beautifulness*). Remember, they're from the French, *beau*, so make sure they're spelled <u>beau</u>.

16. beside – besides

beside = alongside, near the side of

> I sat <u>beside</u> Ida.

besides = in addition to, as well as

> <u>Besides</u> me, Michael and Jeff will be there.

17. breath – breathe

> Use Listerine for bad <u>breath</u>. <u>Breathe</u> deeply, tympanist!

18. can – may

can = is capable of; may = is allowed to

> Jon <u>can</u> lift his German shepherd above his head, but he <u>may</u> not.

19. capital – capitol

capital = main, most important, most serious, as in capital city

capitol = the building where the legislative body meets

> The <u>capitol</u> building is in the <u>capital</u> city of Washington, D.C.

20. censer – censor – censure

censer = a container for burning incense

censor = an official who removes objectionable material

censure (verb) = to criticize as blameworthy

censure (noun) = strong judgment, official reprimand

> Tom was <u>censured</u> for <u>censoring</u> the school paper's story on <u>censers</u> that use stinking incense.

21. cite – site – sight

cite = to point out; site = place; sight = something to see

> <u>Cite</u> an example of Will's slovenliness, please! What a spectacular <u>sight</u>! Where will be the <u>site</u> of the new auditorium?

22. collective – collected

collective = together, as a group

> Through their <u>collective</u> efforts, they were able to raise $12.54.

collected = in control of oneself, calm; assembled or gathered together

> Jon is calm and <u>collected</u>.

23. compliment – complement

compliment (noun) = praise

> Jasmine deserved a <u>compliment</u>.

compliment (verb) = to praise

> It is good to <u>compliment</u> energetic workers.

complement (noun) = an angle that can be added to a given angle to form a right angle

> The <u>complement</u> of a 30° angle is no mystery to Kevin.

complement (verb) = to add or to go well with

> That shade of brown <u>complements</u> Fiona's lovely eyes. Ben's brains <u>complement</u> his brawn.

24. conscience – conscientious – conscious

conscience = sense of moral goodness or blameworthiness

Doesn't your <u>conscience</u> bother you, Simon?

conscientious = scrupulous, meticulous

The <u>conscientious</u> student is always prepared!

conscious = having mental faculties undulled by sleep or stupor

Is the patient <u>conscious</u> or unconscious, Ellie?

25. criterion – criterions – criteria

criterion = standard of judgment

The most important <u>criterion</u> is accuracy.

criterions/criteria = standards (plural)

What <u>criteria</u> were used to evaluate the argument papers?

26. decent – descent

decent = respectable

He's a <u>decent</u> person.

descent = family history or the act of going down

The Larsons are of Swedish <u>descent</u>.

The ascent up Mt. Katahdin was rugged, but the <u>descent</u> was even worse.

27. definite + ly = definitely – defiantly

Make sure you spell *definitely* correctly. If you don't your spell-checker might change it to *defiantly*.

28. desert – dessert

desert (noun) = dry, barren, uncultivated, or wild place

desert (verb) = to leave, especially to abandon a military post

deserts (accent on second syllable) = what one deserves (usually used in the plural)

dessert = a sweet dish one eats at the end of a meal

After <u>deserting</u> his post, Tom got his just <u>deserts</u> by being sent to the Owyhee <u>desert</u> without his <u>dessert</u>!

29. device – devise

device = a plan, scheme, invention or contrivance, usually mechanical

devise = to work out or create something through thought

    Paul <u>devised</u> a most wonderful <u>device</u> for identifying tardy students.

30. disburse – disperse

disburse = to pay out; disperse = to break up, scatter, spread

    I <u>disbursed</u> one hundred dollars to Grace for <u>dispersing</u> the crowd of students in front of my classroom.

31. disinterested – uninterested

disinterested = impartial, fair

    The dispute was resolved with the help of a <u>disinterested</u> party.

uninterested = not interested

    Marla is <u>uninterested</u> in Bruce's antics.

32. eligible – legible

eligible = qualified to take part

    Jasmine, Laura, and Jill are <u>eligible</u> for the 30-kilometer race.

legible = readable

    Rick's writing is not very <u>legible</u>.

33. eminent – imminent

eminent = famous, admired, prominent; imminent = likely to happen in the near future

    The <u>eminent</u> author's arrival is <u>imminent</u>.

34. enumerate – remunerate

enumerate = to number off

    Mr. Strohm will <u>enumerate</u> the course requirements.

remunerate = to pay back

    If you lend me $10, I will <u>remunerate</u> you on payday!

35. etc. = et cetera = and so on

    It's etc. *not* ect.

36. every day – everyday

every day = each day; everyday = typical, usual, common

> Jazz wears <u>everyday</u> clothes <u>every day</u> except Sunday or when she performs in a concert.

37. farther – further

farther = more distant in space; further (verb) = to advance

> We needed to drive <u>farther</u> down the road so we could <u>further</u> our journey.

38. feat – feet – fete

feat = an accomplishment; feet = extremities at the end of your legs

> Running two miles in nine minutes is a <u>feat</u> that requires great stamina (and strong <u>feet</u>).

fete = a celebration or party

> The <u>fete</u> is at Pete's.

39. fewer – less

Use *fewer* for things that can be counted and *less* for amounts that cannot be counted.

40. flair – flare

flare = something that blazes

> The stranded boat sent up a <u>flare</u>.

flair = a natural talent or ability

> Montel has a <u>flair</u> for the dramatic.

41. flaunt – flout

flaunt = to show off; flout = to mock, to openly disregard

> Fiona <u>flouted</u> the school rules by <u>flaunting</u> her singing ability in the library.

42. foreword – forward

forward = toward or at the front

> The project will move <u>forward</u> when funding is available.

foreword = an introductory statement

> Richard Sterling wrote the <u>foreword</u> to this book.

43. good – well

good (adjective) = favorable, positive; well (adverb) = with skill or in a good manner

> I feel like a <u>good</u> person when I do things <u>well</u>.

44. hoping – hopping

hope + ing = hoping; hop + ing = hopping

45. I – me – myself

Myself should *not* be used as a substitute for *me*. *Incorrect usage:* He told Jan and <u>myself</u>.

Use *myself* in two cases:

When the actor and the person receiving the action are the same.

> I asked <u>myself</u> the same question.

When you want to emphasize the action of the subject.

> I painted the deck <u>myself</u>.

Me is never used as the subject of a sentence. *I* rather than *me* should be used after forms of *be*.

> The winner was <u>I</u>.

46. illegible – ineligibile

illegible = unreadable; ineligible = not qualified to compete

> Frank was <u>ineligible</u> for the job because his application was <u>illegible</u>.

47. imply – infer

imply = to suggest without stating implicitly; infer = to arrive at a conclusion based on evidence

> I <u>implied</u> that Steven would not be able to complete his homework, and he <u>inferred</u> my meaning.

48. in – into

in = inside of; into = from the outside to the inside of

> Once you get <u>into</u> the house, then you are <u>in</u> it.

49. incredible – incredulous

incredible = unbelievable, unusual

> Hannah's jump shot is <u>incredible</u>.

incredulous = unable to believe; showing disbelief

> When I told my dad I didn't know how the dent in the fender got there, he gave me an <u>incredulous</u> stare.

50. ingenious – ingenuous

ingenious = gifted with genius and capacity; ingenuous = simple and naïve

> Jasmine's trick was <u>ingenious</u>; Brad was <u>ingenuous</u> to believe she could really walk on water.

51. it's – its

it's = it is; its = possessive form of *it*

> <u>It's</u> a sad day when a dog can't find <u>its</u> tail.

52. lay – lie

lay = to put or to place

lie = to stretch out or recline

53. lens – lenses

> A monocular has only one <u>lens</u>. Binoculars have two <u>lenses</u>.

54. loose – lose

loose = free, unbound

> Free-range chickens run <u>loose</u> and are not confined to cages.

lose = to misplace, to be unable to find

> When did you <u>lose</u> your backpack?

55. media – medium

media = plural; medium = singular

> Television is one <u>medium</u> of communication. There are many <u>media</u>.

56. miner – minor

> <u>Miners</u> work underground. <u>Minors</u> are people who are not of legal age.

57. morning – mourning

morning = when the sun rises and we eat breakfast; mourning = grieving and feeling sad, often for something that has vanished

Tomorrow <u>morning</u> we will begin a period of official <u>mourning</u> for the president's death.

58. pair – pear – pare

pair = two items (often used to refer to an item with two corresponding appendages)

I have a <u>pair</u> of sunglasses and a <u>pair</u> of tennis balls.

pear = a fruit

Pick a <u>pear</u> from the tree, but be careful of the partridge!

pare = to peel

Can you <u>pare</u> an apple for me?

59. passed – past

He <u>passed</u> the ball. I <u>passed</u> the test. She <u>passed</u> out. I <u>passed</u> your house on my way home, Tucker. I <u>passed</u> up that broken-down Honda. I went <u>past</u> your house at 6 p.m., Tucker. All this is in Brad's <u>past</u>.

60. peace – piece

Kate needs <u>peace</u> and quiet. I will definitely have a <u>piece</u> of the pear pie.

61. pedals – petals

My bike needs new <u>pedals</u>. Flowers have <u>petals</u>.

62. picture – pitcher

That is a <u>picture</u> of Jasmine when she was a softball <u>pitcher</u>.

63. precede – proceed

precede = to go before

The superior seniors will <u>precede</u> the judicious juniors.

proceed = to move forward

<u>Proceed</u> to Room 113!

64. principal – principle

principal (noun) = school official; principal (adjective) = main

> The <u>principal</u> gave us detention. Miles's <u>principal</u> sport is soccer.

principle = rule

> Jasmine believes in the <u>principle</u> of nonviolence.

65. raise – rise

raise = to move something to a higher level; rise = to get up, to assume a more upright position

> A key to using these words correctly is remembering that *raise* requires an object (e.g., <u>raise</u> your hand) and *rise* can't take an object.

66. role – roll

role = character or part in a play, or pattern of behavior

> Fiona was sensational in the <u>role</u> of Juliet.

roll = (noun) bread or sweet cake, an official list; (verb) to move in a circular manner

> Have a sweet <u>roll</u>, like a honey bun. I must now call <u>roll</u>, students! Fiona was good at <u>rolling</u> her kayak up once she was upside down.

67. scared – scarred

scared, from scare = to be afraid; scarred, from scar = to leave a mark

> When Mark first got his <u>scar</u>, he was <u>scared</u> that he was <u>scarred</u> for life. But it soon disappeared.

68. scents – sense – since

scents = smells

> Perfumes have pungent <u>scents</u>. A skunk has an acrid <u>scent</u>, much like Paul Corrigan's sweatshirt.

sense = sound mental capacity

> Terry has the good <u>sense</u> not to jump off the bridge.

since = from a point in time

> <u>Since</u> I last talked to you, things have changed.

69. set – sit

set = to put

> Set it down, dummkopf! He's been setting it there for a month. He set it there yesterday. He has always set the quadraped in the corner.

sit = to occupy a seat

> Sit, boy! He sat calmly. He always sat in the front. He's been sitting there since the beginning of school.

70. sole – soul

sole = only; soul = spirit

> Janelle's sole interest is in saving souls.

71. sparing – sparring

sparing, from spare = to save, treat with mercy; sparring, from spar = to punch, hit, box, jab, wrangle, argue, or dispute

> Foreman was sparing with his punches as he sparred with Holeyfield.

72. staring – starring

staring, from stare = to look at; starring, from star = to be featured in, to do well in

> Ashton was staring at a poster for a movie starring Jennifer Lopez.

73. stationary – stationery

stationary = remaining in one place

> Old-fashioned desks at Central High were stationary because they were bolted to the floor!

stationery = writing paper

> The invitation came on official company stationery.

74. striped – stripped

striped, from stripe = a long narrow band or streak

> That's a chic striped skirt, Fraulein! A striped car looks like a race car.

stripped, from strip = to take off

> Big Barry stripped off his sweatsuit, exposing his muscles. A stripped car has nothing inside or outside—it is a shell!

75. than – then

Than is used in comparisons; *then* is related to time.

> Are juniors more judicious <u>than</u> sophomores? <u>Then</u> I decided to rest.

76. that – which

That introduces a clause that is essential to the meaning of a sentence.
Which refers to inanimate things and animals, or is used with clauses that
are nonessential.

> The horse <u>that</u> sings is the horse for me. But horses cannot sing, <u>which</u>
> everyone knows.

77. their – there – they're

their = belonging to them; there = a place; they're = they are

> <u>Their</u> house is over <u>there</u>, but <u>they're</u> not home.

78. threw – through

> He <u>threw</u> the ball <u>through</u> the window. Go <u>through</u> that door.

79. to – too – two

too = very, also; two = the number; to = everything else

> Because I ran <u>two</u> miles, I am way <u>too</u> tired <u>to</u> exercise. I want a
> birthday cake, <u>too</u>.

80. uninhabited – uninhibited

uninhabited = without residents

> Bali Ha'i was not <u>uninhabited</u>—people lived there.

uninhibited = without embarrassment

> Successful actresses like Fiona must be <u>uninhibited</u>.

81. use – utilize

utilize = to put to use, but not in the typical way

> People <u>use</u> a spatula to flip eggs, but sometimes they <u>utilize</u> a spatula to
> spread wax on their skis.

82. vial – vile

vial = small vessel for liquids; vile = foul, low, disgusting

    I drank a <u>vial</u> of <u>vile</u>-tasting medicine.

83. wander – wonder

wander = to move about aimlessly

    Don't <u>wander</u> off, Mademoiselle!

wonder = to feel curiosity or doubt

    Do you ever <u>wonder</u> about Will?

84. wear – we're – were – where

wear = (verb) to carry something on your person, especially clothing; (noun) deterioration through use

    <u>Wear</u> your new skirt. That tire shows a lot of <u>wear</u>.

we're = contraction of we are; were = past tense of was; where = indicates place

    <u>We're</u> ready. We <u>were</u> late. <u>Where</u> are you going, Mademoiselle?

85. weather – whether

    A meterologist knows the <u>weather</u>. Do you know <u>whether</u> he has heard the new recording of *Also Sprach Zarathustra*?

86. which – witch

    <u>Which</u> <u>witch</u> was Glinda in *The Wizard of Oz*?

87. who's – whose

who's = who is/has; whose = belonging to who

    <u>Who's</u> riding the bike? <u>Who's</u> been practicing the Schubert solo? <u>Whose</u> leg was twisted while she was skiing?

88. woman – women

woman = singular; women = plural

    Among all <u>women</u>, I prefer the <u>woman</u> named Peggy Jo!

89. your – you're

your = belonging to you; you're = you are

    If <u>you're</u> very tall, <u>your</u> head may hit the door frame.

APPENDIX C
Sensorium Examples

Read the three examples of sensoriums below. Be prepared to define a sensorium and identify some of its unique features. Also rank these three from best to worst, and be able to justify your reasoning with specific ideas about what a sensorium must do and include.

Kickapoo

Kickapoo, once an Indian tribe and now a convenience store/gas station. For the city of Marysville, Kickapoo is not just a store, but the sole gathering spot for people of all ages. That probably gives you an idea of the sophistication of our wonderful town.

As I near the heavy glass door, I take my hands out of my heavy trench coat's pockets. I reach for the handle and the sweat causes my hand to cling to the cold aluminum. I thrust the door open and the smell of heat comes from a round turbine-like blower on the ceiling. It smells stuffy and stale. Beside the heat comes the overwhelming smell of pizza. I take just a few steps to the pizza booth and look at that pizza! Nice thin crust, hearty seasoned sauce, double dose of real mozzarella cheese, and Lang's fresh Italian sausage. I can just taste the cheese, the sausage, the . . .

AWWWMIGOSHDARNITALL!

I wheel around to see the young chef sucking on his finger. His shin-length apron is flapping as he dances around. I look away and turn toward the slush machine.

VERRVVVVVVERRRRRRRVVVVVVERRRRRR is the sound coming from the original "Slush Puppy" maker. This is a big white box that looks like a small freezer. You have over there, in the rack, your three different flavors of syrup in little pump-bottles; raspberry, cherry, and grape. Now look over here. Here in the center is a lever that you pull to get the slush. I snatch a cup from the shelf and abruptly place it under the spout and yank the handle.

SSSPPPPLISSHASTOMP!

Everyone looks at me and I grin back. Slush is clinging all over me and is spread all over the floor, already melting under the fluorescent lights.

"Clean it up now, huh?" comes a disembodied voice from an overweight, overmade-up, so out-of-style girl who probably will work at Kickapoo the rest of her life. She has on highwater pin-striped jeans that just don't flatter her body type all that well.

I clean up the mess in a jiffy. So what if there is still water on the floor, and I head out the door and out of Kickapoo.

Ted Walks the Line of Life

"POPCORN! RED HOTS! Get your popcorn, red hots!" The vendor with the candy-striped coat struggles up and down the sticky aisles selling his goods. You can hear his feet against the wooden steps and the gluey stretch when he steps out of old Coke spillage.

"Ladies and Gentelllllmennnn!!!" intones the Ring Leader with his deep baritone wavering voice that crackles like electricity through the smoky air of the circus tent.

You can smell the aroma of the luscious, buttered kernels of corn rampaging up your nose so that your nose hairs tremble with delight as the vendor meanders by your seat, so hard and oaken against your butt, which is just beginning to itch and go numb. The salty fragrance of the piping-hot hot dogs makes your mouth water to the point where you swallow down your saliva and you feel the roof of your mouth feel sandy and dry like a Saharan wind and you start thinking of the only thing that can satisfy you and save your right mind: YES! A nice, icy, cold, crisp, cooling Coca-Cola! The thought of this only savior makes you gulp with anticipation as you watch the short plump man in the turquoise vest take out a Styrofoam goblet from his tray.

"In RING NUMBER ONE," announces the Ring Leader, "please give your attention to 'Tight-Rope Ted'!"

You take your eyes off the Ring Leader with his bright red coat and coattails and the silky, pitch-black top hat poised upon his head like a witch's cat, standing tall. Your wide, dish-shaped eyes travel up his pointing arm and take off from his fingertips and ascend like a jet plane up into the atmosphere to the massive elevation of eighty feet above the hard-packed, sawdust-strewn dirt floor below.

"OHHHHHHHH," the crowd shrieks and the girl next to you holds her hand over her heart as if she is having a heart attack and you see tears in the corners of her eyes.

The six-year-old hyperactive kid next to you yells: "Do you see THAT!!??"

You turn around with a grimace on your face that makes the kid shut his mouth and sink in his seat in fear of you in addition to the fear which he now holds inside his metallic, beating brainpan for the safety of Tight-Rope Ted.

You return your attention to the brave madman upon the narrow wire stretched through the sky, which is all that separates his life from death. You note that with each move Ted makes, he is affected by the breath of the terrified crowd. He is thinking that the only thing keeping him balanced on the "wire of life" is the equal intensity of attention that is being paid to him from both sides of the tent. He takes one step—BAM goes the deafening proclamation from the depths of the giant copper circus drums. Ted has his arms spread like an eagle about to fly for his first time as he steps off of the platform and into the space filled only with the thinnest of wires. BAM BAM BAM. Will he fall? He starts to hop across the thin line. He wavers. He balances. BAM BAM BAM BAM BAM. He reaches the other side like a drowning man reaching the far-off shore.

"AHHHHHHHH," the crowd breathes in relief, and you being to feel your parched throat and think again about that icy Coke.

The Gym

ATTENTION: YOU MUST HAVE A MEMBERSHIP CARD TO ENTER. ONE TOWEL PER PERSON. WE WILL NOT HOLD KEYS OR WALLETS. WE WILL NOT TAKE MESSAGES. WE WILL NOT MICROWAVE YOUR FOOD.

That is the sign above Alice as you enter into the gym.

Alice is the receptionist and every time someone asks her a favor she adds it to the sign's list of things she will not do.

She sits behind a yellow desk in a yellow chair which complements her yellow hair. She is perky and likes to move around in her roller chair as she gives out keys and yellow towels.

You walk through the lounge, which has orange couches and yellow chairs and several televisions all tuned in to different stations and all on mute. Several guys sit around watching the television with a tennis match on it. They look mesmerized, at one with the cosmic existence of the world.

You go into the locker room and it smells like sweat and sauna cedar. You hear the clanging of lockers opening and closing, the snapping of Master Locks.

You can hear the showers going and people talking.

You wonder if anyone will show up to play basketball or whether you will have to ride the exercise bike and lift weights. For some reason, riding the exercise bike depresses you.

You walk out in to the gym and hear the dribbling of a ball. Maybe it is your lucky day, maybe there is someone here to play basketball with. Then again, maybe it is that 80-year-old guy who fought in World War I.
You go out into the gym to see.

APPENDIX D
Resources

Here are some resources that we have found useful in thinking about the issues we raise in this book.

Anderson, Jeff. (2005). *Mechanically inclined: Building grammar, usage, and style into writer's workshop.* Portland, ME: Stenhouse.

> A middle school English teacher for many years, Anderson situates short, daily instruction in grammar and mechanics within writing workshop. Includes visual scaffolds and short, regular routines for editing.

Killgallon, Don, and Killgallon, Jenny. (2006). *Grammar for middle school: A sentence-composing approach. A student worktext.* Portsmouth, NH: Heinemann.

> The authors demonstrate how to teach 14 grammatical structures through sentence-combining—a research-supported method of improving sentence structure.

Noden, Harry. (1999). *Image grammar: Using grammatical structures to teach writing.* Portsmouth, NH: Heinemann.

> Noden's book is based on the premise that writers "paint" images, using grammatical structures as tools. Each chapter includes examples from mentor texts as well as teaching strategies and classroom-tested lessons.

Schuster, Edgar. (2003). *Breaking the rules: Liberating writers through innovative grammar instruction.* Portsmouth, NH: Heinemann.

> With an engaging style and a sense of humor, Schuster debunks the often cited but rarely observed "mythrules," identifies the "unbreakable" rules, and shows how to teach them in memorable ways.

Shaughnessy, Mina P. (1977). *Errors and expectations: A guide for the teacher of basic writing.* New York: Oxford University Press.

> A classic that's still fresh and relevant 30 years after its publication, this book was inspired by Shaughnessy's experience teaching underprepared col-

lege writers who entered the New York university system under open admissions. Shaughnessy identifies patterns of errors and then addresses them in ways that are applicable to middle and high school teachers as well.

Weaver, Constance. (2007). *The grammar plan book: A guide to smart teaching.* Portsmouth, NH: Heinemann.

Weaver's latest offering on grammar includes a framework for effective grammar instruction within a workshop structure and a minimal handbook that also serves as a lesson planner.

Weaver, Constance. (1996). *Teaching grammar in context.* Portsmouth, NH: Heinemann.

After examining the ineffectiveness of traditional grammar instruction, Weaver addresses how to teach key grammatical concepts, style, the power of dialects, and punctuation and mechanics.

References

Anderson, J. (2005). *Mechanically inclined.* Portland, ME: Stenhouse.

Bereiter, C. (2004). Reflections on "depth." In *Teaching for deep understanding* (pp. 8–12). Toronto: Elementary Teachers' Federation of Toronto and Ontario Institute for Studies in Education of the University of Toronto.

Bereiter, C., & Scardamalia, M. (1987). *The psychology of written composition.* Hillsdale, NJ: Erlbaum.

Borges, Jorge Luis. (1952/1975). "The Analytical Language of John Wilkins." In *Other inquisitions: 1937–1952.* Austin: University of Texas Press. Retrieved January 28, 2007 from http://www.themodernword.com/borges/borges_quotes.html

Braddock, R., Lloyd-Jones, R., & Schoer, L. (1963). *Research in written composition.* Champaign, IL: National Council of Teachers of English.

Brown, J., Collins, A., & Duguid, P. (1989). Situated cognition and the culture of learning. *Educational Researcher, 18*(1), 32–42.

Bruner, J. (1987). *Actual minds, possible worlds.* Cambridge, MA: Harvard University Press.

Cisneros, S. (1984). *The house on Mango Street.* New York: Vintage Books.

College Board. (n.d.). *Scoring guide.* Retrieved January 29, 2007, from http://www.collegeboard.com/student/testing/sat/about/sat/essay_scoring.html

Connors, R. J., & Lunsford, A. (1988). Frequency of formal errors in current college writing, or Ma and Pa Kettle do research. *College Composition and Communication, 39*(4), 395–409.

Daiker, D., Kerek, A., & Morenberg, M. (1982). *The writer's options: Combining to composing.* New York: Harper & Row.

Delpit, L. (1997). Ebonics and culturally responsive instruction. *Rethinking Schools, 12*(1). Retrieved March 7, 2006, from http://www.rethinkingschools.org/archive/12_01/ebdelpit.shtml

Elley, W. B., Barham, I. H., Lamb, H., & Wyllie, M. (1976). The role of grammar in a secondary school English curriculum. *Research in the Teaching of English, 10,* 5–21.

Erikson, E. (1963). *Childhood and society* (2nd ed.). New York: Norton.

Fu, D. (2003). *An island of English: Teaching ESL in Chinatown.* Portsmouth, NH: Heinemann.

Gee, J. (2003). *What video games have to teach us about learning and literacy.* New York: Palgrave Macmillan.

Goodlad, J. (1984). *A place called school.* New York: McGraw-Hill.

Haneda, M., & Wells, G. (2000). Writing in knowledge-building communities. *Research in the Teaching of English, 34,* 430–457.

Hardy, B. (1977). Towards a poetics of fiction: An approach through narrative. In M. Meek, A. Warlow, & G. Barton (Eds.), *The cool web* (pp. 12–33). London: The Bodley Head.

Hartwell, P. (1985). Grammar, grammars, and the teaching of grammar. *College English, 47,* 105–127.

Haussamen, B. (1997). *Revising the rules: Traditional grammar and modern linguistics* (2nd ed.). Dubuque, IA: Kendall/Hunt.

Hillocks, G., Jr. (1986). *Research on written composition: New directions for teaching.* Urbana, IL: Education Resources Information Center and National Council of Teachers of English.

Hillocks, G., Jr., & Smith, M. W. (2003). Grammars and literacy learning. In J. Flood, J. Jensen, D. Lapp, & J. Squire (Eds.), *Handbook of research on teaching the English language arts* (2nd ed., pp. 721–737). Mahwah, NJ: Erlbaum.

Hook, J. N., & Evans, W. H. (1982). *The teaching of high school English* (5th ed.). New York: Wiley.

Kolln, M., & Funk, R. (1998). *Understanding English grammar* (5th ed.). Needham, MA: Allyn & Bacon.

Krakauer, J. (1996). *Into the wild.* New York: Villard.

Labov, W., Baker, B., Bullock, S., Ross, L., & Brown, M. (1998). A graphemic-phonemic analysis of the reading errors of inner city children. Retrieved March 7, 2006, from University of Pennsylvania, Department of Linguistics: http://www.ling.upenn.edu/~wlabov/Papers/GAREC/GAREC.html

Lindemann, E. (2001). *A rhetoric for writing teachers* (4th ed.). New York: Oxford University Press.

Linguistic Society of America. (1997). LSA resolution on the Oakland "Ebonics" issue. Retrieved March 7, 2006, from https://lsadc.org/info/lsa-res-ebonics.cfm

Lunsford, A. (2008). *The St. Martin's Handbook* (6th ed.). Boston: Bedford/St. Martin's.

Lunsford, A., & Lunsford, K. (2006). 20 most common errors. Retrieved December 9, 2006, from http://bcs.bedfordstmartins.com/easywriter3e/20errors

Macauley, W. J. (1947). The difficulty of grammar. *British Journal of Educational Psychology, 17,* 153–162.

Macrorie, K. (1988). *The I-Search paper.* Portsmouth, NH: Heinemann.

Monahan, M. B. (2001). Raising voices: How sixth graders construct authority and knowledge in argumentative essays. Unpublished doctoral dissertation, Rutgers University.

National Council of Teachers of English. (2003). NCTE resolution on "Students' Rights to Their Own Language." Retrieved March 7, 2006, from http://www.ncte.org

Nickerson, R. S. (1985). Understanding understanding. *American Journal of Education, 93*, 201–239.

Noden, H. (1999). *Image grammar: Using grammatical structures to teach writing.* Portsmouth, NH: Heinemann.

Nurnberg, M. (1972). *Questions you always wanted to ask about English (but were afraid to raise your hand).* New York: Washington Square Press.

O'Neil, W. (1997). If Ebonics isn't a language then tell me what is. *Rethinking Schools, 12*(1). Retrieved March 7, 2006, from http://www.rethinkingschools.org/archive/12_01/eboneil.shtml

Online Writing Lab, Purdue University. The use and nonuse of articles. Retrieved April 20, 2007 from http://owl.english.purdue.edu/handouts/esl/eslart.html#count

Perkins, D. N. (1986). *Knowledge as design.* Hillsdale, NJ: Erlbaum.

Reid, W. (1991). *Verb and noun number in English: A functional explanation.* New York: Longman.

Reid, W. (2004). Monosemy, homonymy and polysemy. In E. Contini-Morava, R. S. Kirsner, B. Rodriguez-Bachiller (Eds.), *Cognitive and communicative approaches to linguistic analysis* (pp. 93–129). Amsterdam/Philadelphia: John Benjamins.

Robinson, A., & Katzman, J., et al. (2005). *Cracking the new SAT.* New York: Princeton Review Publishing.

Roethke, T. (1946). The old florist. In *The collected poems of Theodore Roethke.* New York: Doubleday.

Rolon, J. J. (2004). Are our words ours? A study of discourses in the academic writing of community college Puerto Rican ESL students. Unpublished doctoral dissertation, Rutgers University.

Scholes, R. (1981). *The practice of writing*. New York: St. Martin's.

Schrank, J. (1979). *Snap, crackle and write*. Skokie, IL: National Textbook Company.

Schuster, E. (2003). *Breaking the rules: Liberating writers through innovative grammar instruction*. Portsmouth, NH: Heinemann.

Shaughnessy, M. P. (1977). *Errors and expectations: A guide for the teacher of basic writing*. New York: Oxford University Press.

Shepherd, R., & MacDonald, J. (1975). *Grammar lives*. Evanston, IL: McDougal, Littell & Co.

Smith, M. W. (1991). Evaluation as instruction: Using analytic scales to increase students' composing ability. *Middle School Journal, 22*(1), 20–25.

Smith, M. W., Cheville, J., & Hillocks, G., Jr. (2006). "I guess I'd better watch my English": Grammar and the teaching of English language arts. In C. MacArthur, S. Graham, & J. Fitzgerald (Eds.), *Handbook on writing research* (pp. 263–274). New York: Guilford Press.

Smith, M. W., & Hillocks, G., Jr. (1988). Sensible sequencing: Developing knowledge about literature text by text. *English Journal, 77*(6), 44–49.

Smith, M. W., & Wilhelm, J. (2002). *"Reading don't fix no Chevys": Literacy in the lives of young men*. Portsmouth, NH: Heinemann.

Smith, M. W., & Wilhelm, J. (2006). *Going with the flow: How to engage boys (and girls) in their literacy learning*. Portsmouth, NH: Heinemann.

Stine, R. L. (2003). *A shocker on Shock Street*. New York: Scholastic.

Stine, R. L. (1996). *Ghost camp*. New York: Scholastic.

Strong, W. (1973). *Sentence combining: A composing book*. New York: Random House.

Truss, L. (2003). *Eats, shoots & leaves: The zero tolerance approach to punctuation.* New York: Gotham Books.

Warriner, J. (1982). *Warriner's English grammar and composition: Third course.* Orlando, FL: Harcourt Brace Jovanovich.

Wilhelm, J. (2001). *Improving comprehension with think-aloud strategies.* New York: Scholastic.

Wilhelm, J. (2003). *Action strategies for deepening comprehension.* New York: Scholastic.

Wilhelm, J. (2004). *Reading IS seeing.* New York: Scholastic.

Wilhelm, J. (2007). *Engaging readers and writers with inquiry.* New York: Scholastic.

Wilhelm, J., Baker, T., & Dube-Hackett, J. (2001). *Strategic reading: Guiding the lifelong literacy of adolescents.* Portsmouth, NH: Heinemann.

Index